# STUDENTS' GLOSSARY

OF

# SCOTTISH LEGAL TERMS

BY

## ANDREW DEWAR GIBB, LL.B.

ADVOCATE AND BARRISTER-AT-LAW

REGIUS PROFESSOR OF LAW IN THE
UNIVERSITY OF GLASGOW

Author of *The International Law of Jurisdiction*
*The Law of Collisions on Land*
*A Preface to Scots Law, etc.*

W.  GREEN  &  SON  LTD.
EDINBURGH
1946

A

*First Published* 1946
*Reprinted* 1971, 1975, 1978
*ISBN No.* 0 414 00538 4

*Printed by photo-litho in Great Britain by*
LINDSAY & CO. LTD., EDINBURGH
*for*
W. GREEN & SON, LTD.

*Made in Great Britain*

# INTRODUCTION

In every legal system there are terms of art which must necessarily puzzle the layman. Included in the term layman is the young man beginning the study of law. It is too often taken for granted by those who instruct him that the student knows the meaning of the curious words and expressions which are part of the teacher's normal vocabulary. That however is far from being the case, and as a result a good many lawyers go through life with a hazy or even a wrong idea of the sense of certain expressions. What meaning for example could the novice take out of the statement in a students' text-book that " the only passive title in moveables is vitious intromission," without a previous explanation of " passive title " ?

Perhaps this little book, based on recognised authorities, and written, it is hoped, in reasonably intelligible terms, may go some way towards improving that state of matters. It may be too that others than students who have to wrestle with the meaning of the *voces signatae* of Scots Law will find it useful.

The book is concerned almost exclusively with legal expressions which are truly and exclusively lawyers' expressions. It does not purport to explain words which are part of lay language and reasonably well understood, such as " contract," " murder," " condition," and the like. Thus delimited, the collection consists mainly of words peculiar to Scots Law or which have a peculiar meaning attached to them by Scots Law. The separation of lawyer's and layman's language in Scotland is the more acute because a Scots lawyer may have a technical term for the expression of some idea which the layman usually expresses by an English word that is at once a lawyer's and a layman's word. Thus a Scottish layman uses the word " bankruptcy " which is the English popular *and technical* word. Few Scots laymen would use " sequestration " which, however, is the correct legal expression for bankruptcy in Scotland. Again, for every Scotsman who speaks of " confirmation," there are ten who will use " probate."

This Scottish legal vocabulary is interesting and fairly extensive. It has a number of components which vary in quality and origin. Thus there is the English term (legal or lay) with a special meaning, like " embezzle." There is the word drawn from the Scottish language, like " thole " or the Scots variant of an English term, like " assignation." There is also a class of words which, so to speak, simulate English words but which are simply unknown in English or at least in modern English ; for example " approbate " or " stellionate." It is the vocabulary consisting of all these classes of words and expressions that is to be found in this Glossary.

A. D. G.

*September* 1946.

*List of Abbreviations will be found on p. 96*

# A

**Abbreviate.**
(i) Of adjudication. An abstract of a decree of adjudication (*q.v.*) containing the names of debtor and creditor, the lands adjudged and the amount of the debt registered as a necessary step in the process of adjudication.
(ii) In bankruptcy; an abbreviate or abstract of the petition for sequestration and the first deliverance must be registered. Other abbreviates are known in bankruptcy proceedings.

**Absolvitor.**
The judgement pronounced when a Court assoilzies: *q.v.*

**Abstracted multures.**
See *Multures*.

**Acceptilation.**
Extinction of debt by an arrangement which falls short of full performance.

**Accession.**
Natural or artificial addition to existing things whereby additional property is acquired, as, *e.g.*, the young of animals, or a new house.

**Accession. Deed of**
A deed executed by the creditors of an insolvent, approving and accepting an arrangement by him for settling his affairs.

**Accessory action.**
An action which subserves an ulterior legal purpose as, *e.g.*, proving of the tenor, in order later to base a claim upon the deed set up by the action.

**Accessory obligation.**
An obligation undertaken in order to render an earlier obligation more effective as, *e.g.*, a cautionary obligation.

**Account charge and discharge.**
An account, usually annual, of the intromissions of factors, executors, trustees and the like, or their agents, with the property committed to their care.

**Accountant of Court.**
An officer of Court who supervises the conduct of judicial factors and others.

**Accretion.**
(i) When the imperfect title of A, who has conveyed to B, is later perfected in A, this validation " accresces " to and perfects B's title.
(ii) Occurs in the case of joint legatees when one dies and his share goes or accresces to the others.

5

**Acredale.**

Archaic term for lands let out in sections to villagers

**Act and Warrant.**

The interlocutor in sequestration proceedings which confirms the appointment of the trustee. Erskine, Pr. IV., 1A., 9.

**Act of Grace.**

The Act 1696, c. 32, which relieved royal burghs from the burden of alimenting civil prisoners, was so called.

**Acts of Adjournal.**

Regulations as to procedure made by the High Court of Justiciary in virtue of statutory power.

**Acts of Sederunt.**

Procedural rules made by the judges of the Court of Session in virtue of statutory power.

**Actings.**

A favourite but unnecessary synonym for " acts " or " conduct."

*Ad remanentiam.*

See *Resignation.*

**Adhere.**

This word means (i) of husband or wife, to remain with and be faithful (to the other); (ii) of a court, to affirm the judgement of a lower court.

**Adjudication.**

A process used to attach heritable property. Formerly it was used by a disponee of land against a person who would have been heir and who refused to grant him a title. This was *adjudication in implement* and is obsolete. Adjudication may be used to-day in *implement of sale* : *i.e.,* where a seller of land refuses to give a conveyance to the buyer. Or it may be used as a means of taking a debtor's land to satisfy his creditor's claim for debt. To *lead an adjudication* is to put an adjudication in force.

**Adjust.**

To alter the averments or pleas in a written pleading, before the record is closed.

**Adminicle.**

A piece of supporting or corroborative evidence. Stair has *adminiculate,* a verb : IV., 42, 19.

**Administration. Right of**

The right of the husband, now abolished, to manage the property of his wife, in virtue of which his consent to all her legal acts was essential. Often used in its Latin form of *jus administrationis.*

6

**Administrator at law.**
A title given to a father (and to the mother *qua tutrix*) in his relationship to his children who are under 21.

**Admiral. Lord High**
Once Commander of the Naval forces of Scotland. He had too a civil and criminal jurisdiction which was administered by the Judge Admiral. All now abolished.

**Advise.**
To advise is to give a considered judgement in a case. See *Avizandum*.

**Advocate.**
(i) A member of the Scottish Bar ; also a solicitor who is a member of the Society of Advocates in Aberdeen. And see *Lord Advocate.*
(ii) As a verb, to bring up the judgement of an inferior court for review : now incompetent in civil cases : competent but rare in criminal cases. See MacDonald, 578.

**Advocate-depute.**
An advocate appointed by the Lord Advocate to prosecute under his directions, and paid by salary.

**Aemulatio vicini.**
Spite against one's neighbour which, if a motive, may render unlawful an act which is normally within a man's legal power.

**Agent.**
See *Law agent.*

**Aggravation.**
Some circumstance in a criminal charge, as, *e.g.*, a previous conviction, which, if proved, renders conviction more serious.

**Agnate.**
Agnates are persons related through the father.

**Aliment.**
Support or maintenance of a wife or relative enforceable by law. The word is also used as a verb.

**Alimentary.**
Of the nature of or by way of aliment, as a fund or payment. The word connotes freedom from the claims of creditors.

**Allenarly.**
Only. Important when associated with a liferent as preventing the liferent from being construed as a fee.

**Allodial.**
Non-feudal, as applied to the tenure of land, as in the case of *udal tenure (q.v.)* and church property. Erskine, Pr. II., iii., 4.

7

**Allowance of an apprising.**
A decree in confirmation of an apprising (*q.v.*) written on the back by the clerk to the bills. Bell. Obs.

**Alluvion.**
Gradual accretion to land caused by the action of a river. The owner of the land which is increased benefits.

*Altius non tollendi.*
The name given to a servitude which prevents the servient owner from building beyond a certain height on his own ground.

**Amand.**
A penalty. Archaic.

**Amend. To**
To make an alteration on pleadings after the record is closed.

**Ann, annat.**
A half-year's stipend payable to the nearest of kin of a minister after his death, under the Act 1672, c. 13.

**Annual rent.**
Interest on money lent. So called because when, before the Reformation interest was illegal, a sum derived from land was made payable by way of evasion. Bell.

**Annuity.**
The right to a yearly payment in money.

*Annus deliberandi.*
The year and day accorded to an apparent heir to decide whether or not to take up his predecessor's estate. Later reduced to 6 months.

**Answer.**
A written pleading given in to a court usually in reply to a claim. Bell.

*Apocha trium annorum.*
Literally, a receipt of three years : three successive periodic payments, raising a presumption of payment of earlier instalments.

**Apparent heir.**
One to whom a succession has actually opened by the death of his predecessor, but who has not completed his title to the estate succeeded to. Compare and contrast *Heir-apparent, infra.*

**Appoint. To**
To order, or direct, as of a court.

**Appraiser.**
A person appointed to value poinded goods.

**Apprehend. To**
The true Scottish term of art for to arrest in a criminal sense.

**Apprising.**
The sentence of a Sheriff by which the heritable rights of a debtor were sold to pay a debt due to the appriser. Erskine, Pr. II., xii., 1.

**Approbate and reprobate.**
Approve or accept or adopt, and disapprove, refuse or reject. It is commonly said that a deed or transaction cannot be approbated and reprobated, *i.e.*, that a party must accept all or reject all.

*Apud acta.*
Literally, at the time of the proceedings ; notice of future proceedings is given *apud acta* when it is given orally at a sitting of the court without written citation. A rare expression.

*Aquaehaustus.*
A servitude under which the servient owner must permit watering cattle or taking water at his ponds or wells.

**Arbiter.**
A person chosen voluntarily by parties to a dispute to decide the difference between them. Not *arbitrator*, as in England.

**Arbitrary punishment.**
Punishment inflicted at the discretion of the judge, either quite arbitrarily or arbitrarily within limits, as are most punishments in the High Court so far as concerns duration of imprisonment. Erskine, Pr. IV., iv., 6.

**Arles.**
Earnest, given in evidence of the engagement of a servant.

**Arrest.**
To arrest, whether in execution, in security or to found jurisdiction, is to take or attach the property of another, debtor or defender, in the hands of a third party. As applied to the person arrest is, in strict Scots usage, apprehend.

**Arrestee.**
The person holding goods which are arrested.

**Arrestment.**
The process of arresting. See *Arrest*.

**Art and part.**
In the capacity of an accessory, or accomplice. The derivation is uncertain ; but the expression means perhaps either by contrivance (art) or actual participation (part). See Hume, ii., 225.

**Articles improbatory and approbatory.**
Pleadings which respectively impugned and sustained a writing in a process in which it was attacked as being false or forged. Bell.

**Articles of Roup.**
See *Roup*.

**Articles. Lord of the**
A standing committee of the Scots Parliament, which at one time alone could initiate legislation.

**Articulate adjudication.**
" A congeries of single adjudications carried on as one action to avoid expense." Bell's Comm., 1, 773.

**As accords of law.**
As is agreeable or conformable to law. Jamieson.
Often shortened to " as accords."

**Ascendant.**
In a question of succession, a person akin to the deceased in a preceding generation.

**Assignation.**
An assigning of rights (as of rents or writs in a disposition) ; or, the instrument by which a right is assigned. *Assignment* is the English expression.

**Assize.**
In Scotland this word is occasionally and formally used to mean a jury. It used to mean also the sittings or the ordinances of a court.

**Assoilzie.**
To absolve or decide finally in favour of a defender.

**Assume.**
To adopt, as of a new trustee.

**Assumption.**
Adoption, as of a new trustee.

**Assythment.**
A sum given to relatives of a person killed, by way of *solatium* and indemnification when the killing amounted to a crime. Obs. Bell's Pr., 2029.

**Astrict.**
To bind lands to a mill so that all grain grown on the lands must be taken to be ground at the mill.

**Astriction.**
A provision astricting or binding tenants to carry their grain to a particular mill.

**Auctor in rem suam.**
Agent for his own advantage ; a rôle which neither agent nor trustee is allowed to assume.

**Attestor.**
One who attests the sufficiency of a cautioner in a suspension.

**Attour.**
Besides, over and above.  Jamieson.

**Auditor.**
The Auditor of Court is the officer who taxes accounts of expenses ; the English *taxing-master*.

**Augmentation.**
An action or process of augmentation is brought in the Teind Court by a parish minister in order to obtain an increase in stipend.

**Author.**
One from whom a man derives his title by sale or gift.

**Avail.**
The avail of marriage was a payment by vassal to superior on the former's attaining puberty.  It was single avail or double according to circumstances.  Abolished by 20 Geo. II., c. 50.

**Aver.**
To state or allege, particularly in written pleadings.

**Averment.**
Statement.  See *Aver*.

**Avizandum.**
Originally in the gerundial phrase, *avizandum est* ; the single word is used as a noun and the Court " makes *avizandum* " when it takes time to consider its judgement.  Cf. the English, *Curia advisari vult*.

**Avulsio.**
Removal of land, by the action of a river, from one situation to another.  Less gradual than *alluvio*, it causes no change of property.

**B**

**Back, or back up**
To endorse, of a folded document.

**Back-bond.**
An instrument which qualifies some other instrument purporting to give an absolute right.  Sometimes *Back-letter*.

**Back-letter.**
See *Back-bond*.

**Bailiary.  Letter of**
The commission which appointed a baron-bailie.  Bell.

11

**Bailie.**

A magistrate in a Scottish burgh. The word also meant the person appointed by a precept of sasine to give infeftment, but this is obsolete.

**Bairns' part of gear.**

Now usually called legitim. It is the part of a parent's moveables to which children are entitled on the parent's death : one-third when the other parent survives, one-half otherwise.

**Bankruptcy**

See *Notour bankruptcy.*

**Bar.**

See *Personal bar.*

**Baron.**

The lowest degree of the nobility. Anciently, every vassal holding land directly under the Crown was a baron and until the fifteenth century sat in Parliament. The titled barons were the *greater,* the others the *lesser barons.*

**Barony.**

The right of a baron or person holding land directly from the Crown. Also applied to the land itself. It formerly involved a considerable jurisdiction, civil and criminal. See Erskine, Pr. I., iv., 25.

**Bankrupt.**

See *Sequestrate.*

**Bannock.**

See *Sequels.*

**Base holding.**

A holding from one not the original superior of a feudal holding. When A feus land to B and B sub-feus to X, the right of X is base.

**Before answer.**

Before the law of a case is decided. Thus when a proof is allowed *before answer,* the facts are brought out, but the legal argument that they do not entitle the person to relief is still competent.

*Benefice.*

A Church living, based upon land. It consisted either of the *spirituality* or teind : or the *temporality,* the land itself. Bell. Erskine, Pr. II., x., 1.

*Beneficium.*

A privilege, benefit or right, as in the expression *beneficium ordinis,* right of " discussion " (*q.v.*) of a principal creditor. *Beneficium discussionis,* right of a cautioner that a co-cautioner share obligation *pro rata ; beneficium competentiae,* right of

12

granter of a gratuitous obligation who is indigent to retain sufficient for his own maintenance ; *beneficium inventarii* gave to an heir the privilege of limitation of his liability for his predecessor's debts to the value contained in the inventory.

### Bill.

A petition presented to the Court of Session asking for the sealing of letters with the King's signet as was necessary in the case of certain " privileged summonses." The Bill was also at one time necessary in suspensions and advocations and in applying for various kinds of diligence. Nominally still competent in a few cases, it is in reality obsolete. Green, II., 171.

### Bill Chamber.

A Court, abolished in 1933, whose name was taken from the bills (*q.v.*) which were presented to it. It dealt with miscellaneous business, such as general vacation work, proceedings in suspensions and the granting of bills for letters passing under the signet. Green, II.

### Black mail.

Payment made to " reivers " for protection against their depredations. Hume, i, 476–477.

### Blank. Bonds in.

Bonds in which the name was left blank and which " passed from hand to hand like notes payable to the bearer." They were rendered null by the Act 1696, c. 25, as facilitating fraud. Erskine, Pr. III., ii., 8.

### Blazon.

The badge of office in brass or silver bearing the King's arms and worn upon the breast by messengers-at-arms. It had to be worn by messengers when arresting debtors. Stair, IV., 47, 14.

### Blench (or less commonly) Blanch.

An epithet (used also adverbially) descriptive of a feudal holding where the reddendo is merely nominal, as, *e.g.*, a rose.

### Blood-wit.

Archaic expression for a riot involving bloodshed.

### Boll.

A measure of grain equal to six bushels. See *Chalder*.

### Bond.

A written obligation to pay money or to do some act, *e.g.*, a *bond of caution* to act as surety for another ; a *bond of corroboration*, fortifying or corroborating an obligation already undertaken ; *bond of presentation* binding the obligor to " present " to the proper officer a person liberated from custody for debt on his undertaking (obs.) ; *bond of relief* by a debtor in favour of his cautioner binding himself to relieve the latter ; *bond and disposition in security*, the commonest form of heritable security, consisting of a personal obligation to pay debt and interest and a disposition of the land in security ; it differs from the *heritable bond*, now disused, in that the latter only gave power to recover payment of the principal sum by entering into possession and drawing the rents whereas under the bond and disposition in security there is a power of sale.  Wood, 459.

### Booking.
A mode of land holding, peculiar to the burgh of Paisley, in which a disponee was secured not by infeftment but by *booking* or registration in a Register of Booking, at one time after formal proceedings in the Council Chamber.  The distinctions between this and the ordinary tenure tend to disappear.

### Books of Adjournal.
The books or records of the Justiciary Court.

### Books of Council and Session.
A popular title for the Registers of Deeds and Probative Writs in which, according to the directions they contain, deeds, etc., may be registered for preservation or preservation and execution.  Green, V., 35.

### Books of Sederunt.
Records of the Acts of Sederunt of the Court of Session.

### Border warrant.
A warrant for the arrest of the effects and person of a man in England for debts owed in Scotland.

### Bounding charter.
One which defines the land comprised in it by description of the boundaries.

### Bowing.
A contract by which A lets out his herd to X (the bower) to be grazed on A's farm.  See Rankine on Leases, 290.

### Box : box-day.
To *box* is to lodge in the office of the Court of Session.
*Box-day*, a day in vacation for lodging papers.

### Brevi manu.
Directly, or by short cut.  *Brevi manu* action is action taken to redress a legal wrong without the interposition of the Court.

### Brieve (also breve).
A warrant from Chancery, authorising an inquest or inquiry by a jury into any one of a variety of questions, such as the appointment of a tutor or the definition of a widow's terce. Now practically obsolete.  Maclaren, C.S.P., 151.  And see *Mortancestry.*

**Brigancy.**
Another name for *Depredation, q.v.*

**Burden.**
In its usual legal sense some limitation, restriction, or encumbrance affecting property.

**Burdensack (also burdinseck, burthynsack).**
An alleged rule of great antiquity, to the effect that a man was not a thief who took, to satisfy hunger, as much meat as he could carry on his back. Not now law.

**Burgage.**
Burgage tenure was the type of holding under which property in royal burghs was held of the Crown. Now obsolete as a separate tenure.

**Burgh (also burrow).**
In addition to its meaning of town this word meant, anciently, a cautioner. See *Lawburrows.*

**Burgh acres.**
Pieces of land near royal burghs often feued out to burgesses or other residents. Bell's Pr., 1099.

**Burgh laws.**
An ancient collection of laws relating to burghs : the *Leges Burgorum.*

## C

**Caduciary.**
An adjective meaning subject or relating to or by way of escheat or lapse—thus Murray. In English use it is *caducary.* Rare.

**Call (of summons).**
A summons is called by the exhibition, in a list on a wall of the Court, of the names of parties and their legal representatives. From this date is reckoned the time for entering appearance.

**Calumny. Oath of**
An oath taken at the outset of an action to the effect that the facts pleaded are believed true. Obsolete except in consistorial cases.

**Cane.**
See *Kain.*

*Capita.* **Succession** *per*
Occurs where the property goes to a number of individuals in equal shares and where no single share is divided amongst several as representing a predecessor, as in succession *per stirpes.*

## Caption. Letters of

A warrant to officers of law or magistrates to apprehend for debt (on the theory that the debtor was a rebel ; see *Thom* v. *Black* 7 S. 158). In desuetude. See *Process caption.*

## Carrucate.

A plough-gate : a very varying measure of land, perhaps a hundred acres (Scots) more or less.

## Case.

See *Information.*

## Cash credit.

An arrangement for a loan whereby the borrower on giving security may draw, up to his limit, what he needs and may repay from time to time, paying interest only on what he actually takes out. It is carried out by a *cash-credit bond.* Menzies, 254.

## Casualty.

A payment falling due to a superior on the happening of events of uncertain date or occurrence : *e.g.*, *relief* (*q.v.*). Now abolished.

## Casual homicide.

An accidental killing involving no fault in the killer.

## Catholic creditor.

One who holds security for his debt over more than one piece of property belonging to his debtor.

## *Casus amissionis.*

The manner in which a writing was lost must be established in an action of proving the tenor. This is called the *casus amissionis.*

## Caution.

Security, in civil matters. *Cautionry* is the obligation by which one becomes surety for another. Caution is pronounced to rhyme with nation.

## Cautioner.

A surety.

## Certification.

" The assurance given to a party of the course to be followed in case he disobeys the will of the summons or other writ or the order of the Court." Bell.

## Certiorate.

To give formal notice of a fact to.

## Cess.

Land tax.

16

## Cessio bonorum.

A process whereby a debtor gave up his whole estate and was in return rendered immune from imprisonment on account of his debts. It was later used as a means of sequestration of small estates. Obs. in both senses.

## Chalder.

A measure of quantity equal to sixteen *bolls* (*q.v.*). Used in estimating ministers' stipends.

## Chamberlain.

The name of a former officer-of-state having the duty of inspecting royal burghs, inquiring into the conduct of magistrates and seeing to the due application of the burgh revenues. The title is also sometimes used to-day of the treasurer of a burgh.

## Chancellor.

Foreman of a jury. There has been no high officer of state with the title of Chancellor in Scotland since 1707.

## Chancery.

An office originally directed by the Lord Chancellor of Scotland, but surviving him. Formerly, questions of property were tried on brieves issuing from the chancery and directing an inferior judge to try some issue with a jury. This is largely obsolete but the chancery has continued to deal with the service of heirs and the recording of services. A so-called *Sheriff of Chancery* was created in 1847 with duties in regard to service and also the revising of Crown Charters, but the office was abolished in 1933. Writs are sealed in the chancery with the Quarter Seal (*e.g.*, gifts of *ultimus haeres*) and commissions (as of the Lord Advocate) are issued, formerly by the *Director of Chancery*, now by the various persons appointed by the Reorganisation of Offices Act of 1928 to take over his duties. See S. R. & O. 1932, No. 148.

## Charge.

Generally, an order to obey a decree of the Court. In conveyancing law the word was used in the expressions, *general charge*, *special charge*, and *general-special charge*, these being writs under the signet for compelling heirs in heritage to take up or renounce the succession so as to enable creditors of the estate to receive satisfaction. Bell's Pr., 1856-7. Now abolished.

In modern civil diligence a charge, which is a pre-requisite of poinding, is a written command in the King's name requiring the debtor to pay or perform in a given time.

## Charge and discharge. Account,

See *Account, charge and discharge.*

17

**Charter.**
A deed granted by a superior for a variety of purposes, as of an original grant of the land, or a re-grant, or entering a purchaser. See *Confirmation, Resignation, Novodamus.*

**Charter by progress.**
The charter of confirmation and the charter of resignation (see both expressions) were called charters by progress because they were used to renew a right previously held, as distinguished from an original charter by which a right was created. Menzies, 599.

*Chaud melle.*
Chance medley. A brawl or *mêlée.* The words were used as the name of a plea entitling to sanctuary. See Hume, i. 240.

**Child stealing.**
See *Plagium.*

*Chirographum apud debitorem repertum.*
A written obligation found in a debtor's possession : these words are used to refer to the presumption of payment which arises from such a fact—*Chirographum apud debitorem repertum praesumitur solutum.*

**Choosing curators (action of).**
An action by which a minor without a curator obtained the appointment of a curator at the hands of the Court. Abolished.

**Circumduction.**
Only in the phrase *circumduction of the term* : the formal closing by interlocutor of the term or period within which evidence of a party's case might be brought. Obs.

**Circumvention.**
See *Facility and circumvention.*

**Circuit court.**
The Court held by the judges of the High Court of Justiciary on their visits to the three circuits.

**Cite.**
To summon to Court, whether of party, witness, or juror.

*Clare constat.* **Precept of**
A deed granted by a superior to the heir of a deceased vassal setting forth that it " clearly appears " that the applicant for the precept is lawful heir. Upon this sasine is taken. A writ of *clare constat* is a later statutory elaboration which has the advantage of confirming all deeds necessary to a good title. See Wood, 534.

**Clause.**

The following names of clauses in deeds are perhaps not self-explanatory and therefore, worth mentioning : a *clause of devolution* is one " devolving " an office or duty on X upon failure of A to do some act ; a *clause of return* is one by which the granter of a right provides that in certain circumstances it shall return or revert to himself ; *clauses irritant and resolutive,* found in entails, rendered void acts done contrary to the provisions of the deed and took away *(resolved)* the rights of the offender.

**Clerk of Justiciary.**

The principal clerk of court in the High Court of Justiciary.

**Clerk Register.  Lord**

This functionary was once an important officer of state, having been at various epochs Keeper of the Great and other Seals, Clerk of Parliament, and custodian of the Registers, to name only these.  He is now shorn of all practical duties except that of presiding over the election of representative Scottish peers.

**Clerk of Session.**

The principal clerk of court in the Court of Session.

**Clerk of Teinds.**

The principal clerk of court in the Teind Court.

**Clerk to the Signet.**

See *Signet.*

**Cognate.**

A relative through the mother.

**Cognition.**

A judicial process by which a man might be found insane and a curator might be appointed.  Competent but rare.  Other uses of cognition are in *cognition and sale,* where tutors obtained authority to sell a pupil's heritage (obsolete) ; *cognition to terce,* whereby the extent of terce was determined (obsolete) ; *cognition and sasine* whereby an heir in burgage property was established in his right and title (obsolete, see *Burgage*).

*Cognitionis causa tantum.*

For the sake of recognition or determination merely.  A decree is *cognitionis causa tantum* when given formally against an heir who declines to take up the succession, since some decree is needed to form the ground of adjudication.  See Erskine, Pr. II., xii., 47.

*Collatio* (or **collation**) *inter haeredes.*

The bringing of heritage into one common stock with the moveables so that the heir in heritage may share in the moveable succession with the heirs in moveables.

**Collatio (or collation) inter liberos.**

Relates to the sum available for legitim—the legitim fund—and is the crediting to that fund of any provision received in advance, during the parents' life, by one who later claims on the fund.

**Collateral.**

In regard to succession, means strictly brothers and sisters. It is sometimes used to include descendants of collaterals and brothers and sisters of ascendants. See Walker's Intestate Succession, p. 30. In regard to securities ; a *collateral security* is an additional and separate security for the due performance of an obligation. The word is not a synonym for security, as in America.

**College of Justice.**

A formal name of the Court of Session. The College of Justice includes advocates, writers to the signet, clerks, and others, as well as the judges.

**Commissary.**

Originally an ecclesiastical judge having jurisdiction in such matters as legitimacy, succession, declarators of marriage. His place has been taken partly by the sheriff, partly by the Court of Session.

**Commission for taking proof.**

A warrant or authorisation by the Court of some qualified person to take the evidence of witnesses. It is always coupled with a diligence which enables witnesses to be cited and documents to be called for.

**Commissioners of supply.**

Persons appointed to collect the Land Tax and apply it for such purposes as payment of schoolmasters and upkeep of roads. Obs.

**Commissioners in a Sequestration.**

Persons, three in number, appointed in a sequestration pursuant to the Bankruptcy Act, 1913, to advise the trustee.

**Commissioners of Teinds.**

The judges of the Court of Session are Commissioners of Teinds, another name for the Teind Court, which exercises ministerial and judicial functions.

**Commissioner. Lord High**

The representative of the Sovereign in the General Assembly of the Church of Scotland.

**Commit.**

To order a man's consignment to prison either to await further enquiry into the case or until he is liberated in due course of law. The latter is known as " fully " committing.

**Communings.**
An expression sometimes used of negotiations leading up to a contract.

**Commixtion.**
Mixture of property belonging to different people with results upon property rights which vary with circumstances. See Gl. and H., 4th Ed., 436.

**Communicate.**
To pass on or hand over, as of some advantage.

**Commodate.**
A loan made gratuitously of an article which must be returned exactly as lent.

**Common agent.**
A solicitor appointed in processes where there are several claimants with common interests as in ranking and sales, locality of stipend and multiple-poindings (*q.o.v.*). He act, for those having common interests.

**Common debtor.**
When A owes money to X which X recovers by arresting in the hands of B a sum due by B to A, A is known as the common debtor.

**Common good.**
Property of a burgh, derived from some other source than the rates.

**Common interest.**
An interest, as of adjoining users of a common wall or floor, not amounting to property, but entitling the party interested to a say in the use of the thing.

**Common property.**
Common ownership in a thing or land, without demarcation of shares and characterised especially by the existence of a right in any common owner to compel a division of the common property.

**Commonty.**
A right (neither common property nor common interest) of joint perpetual use conferred by the proprietor of land for the common use of many. Bell, Pr., 1087. Accounts of commonty vary widely.

**Communicate.**
To make some right available to another in fulfilment of a legal duty.

**Compear.**
Of a defender, to appear in the action.

### Compensatio injuriarum.

A set-off, in defence, of a claim of damages against the pursuer's claim, properly in respect of a wrong of the same kind, which is usually defamation. Bell.

### Competent and omitted.

Pleas which might have been but have not been taken are said to be " competent and omitted." Bell.

### Composition.

(i) A casualty (*q.v.*) payable to a superior by a buyer of land on entering upon the estate as a vassal.

(ii) A proportion of his debts which an insolvent offers to his creditors and which, if accepted and approved by the Court, forms the basis of a settlement without sequestration running its course.

### Comprising.

A process, superseded by adjudication, whereby land might be taken for debt. Wood, 361.

### Conclusion.

The conclusion in a Court of Session summons is the statement of the precise relief sought. *To conclude for* is to claim in this fashion.

### Concourse.

Has two meanings : (*a*) the simultaneous existence of two actions based on the same grounds ; (*b*) the concurrence of the public prosecutor in a private prosecution.

### Concursus debiti et crediti.

In a question of compensation it is necessary that the parties be at the same time, debtor and creditor, one of the other, and debtor and creditor in the same capacity. This is the *concourse of debit and credit.* Gloag on Contract, 646.

### Condescendence.

The part of a pursuer's written pleadings which contains a statement of the facts on which he relies.

### Condictio indebiti.

A term of the Civil Law sometimes used in Scotland, meaning an action for repayment of money paid in error.

### Conditional institute.

See *Institute.*

### Conditio si institutus.

See *Si sine liberis decesserit.*

### Conditio si testator.

See *Si sine liberis decesserit.*

**Confident.**
See *Conjunct and confident.*

**Confirmation.**
Has two meanings : (*a*) in regard to executors, the process whereby they are judicially recognised or confirmed in their office and empowered to act ; (*b*) in the land law, a ratification of the right of a purchaser of land, given to him by the superior through a *charter of confirmation.* Now abolished.

**Conform.**
In conformity. Commonly in the expression *decree conform,* a judgement by one court given to render effective the judgement of another.

**Confusio.**
Commixtion (*q.v.*) of liquids.

**Conjoin.**
To order that two processes involving the same subject-matter and the same parties be tried together.

**Conjunct and confident.**
Related by blood and connected by interest. The phrase, *conjunct and confident persons,* is used by the Act 1621, c. 18, to indicate persons alienations to whom made without true cause by an insolvent, are void.

**Conjunct.**
Joint. Thus, *conjunct fee and liferent* exists where there is a joint fee in two or more during their lives, the survivor taking a fee of one-half with a liferent of the other.

**Conjunct probation or proof.**
The process of disproving by evidence an opponent's averments, carried on as part of the process of proving a party's own case. See Maclaren, C.S.P., 537. And see *Replication. Proof in.*

**Conjunct and several.**
A conjunct and several (or joint and several) obligation is one in which each obligant is singly liable to perform the whole obligation if called on. The obligants are said to be liable *singuli in solidum.*

**Conquest.**
A comprehensive name for the heritage which a man acquired by purchase or gift as opposed to inheritance. In certain cases the heir of conquest was not the same as the heir of line. The distinction was abolished by the Conveyancing Act, 1874.

**Consanguinean.**
A brother or sister is consanguinean with another where they have a common father but different mothers.

### Consistorial.
Is derived from *consistorium*, the place where the Emperor's council met. The bishops used it for their courts and thence the adjective *consistorial* came to be used as descriptive of the court of the commissaries (*q.v.*) and of the actions which were tried there. In modern use, as applied to actions, it has been narrowed down to mean actions between husband and wife which involve status.

### Consolidation.
The vesting in one person of a superiority, or *dominum directum*, of land together with the *dominum utile* or beneficial ownership.

### Constable. Lord High
An ancient officer of state having command of the army on service when the King was not present and possessing also a certain criminal jurisdiction.

### Constitute.
To determine or establish a debt, usually by means of the judgement of a Court. Especially of the case where the action is against heirs for a debt of their predecessor.

### Consult.
Power exists for a Division of the Court of Session to invoke the opinion of or consult other judges in a case where there is especial difficulty or where the judges of the Division are equally divided. See Mackay's Manual, 4.

### Contentation.
An almost obsolete word meaning assent, satisfaction.

### Contingency.
A similarity in the subject-matter of actions which may lead the Court to remit the later in time, *ob contingentiam*, to the Court seised of the earlier.

### Continue.
To postpone decision in judicial proceedings and adjourn them to a later date for further action.

### Contumacy.
A person is guilty of contumacy, or *contumacious*, when he refuses obedience to a legal citation.

### Conventional.
Of obligations, arising out of agreement or contract, as opposed to those imposed by law.

### Convention of Burghs.
An ancient assembly of representatives of burghs, which still meets annually to discuss matters of burghal and even national interest.

24

**Convention of Estates.**

A convening of the Scottish Estates in an emergency without the procedure normally required for summoning Parliament. Naturally obsolete.

**Count and reckoning. Action of**

An action brought to compel a person in the position of an agent to give an account of his dealing with property under his control, and pay any balance found due. Maclaren, C.S.P., 654.

**Courtesy.**

The liferent enjoyed by a widower of the heritage of his late wife.

**Crave.**

To ask formally of a Court. This unpleasantly abject word is also used as a noun : in Sheriff Court practice part of the initial writ, for example, is called the *crave*.

**Crimen falsi.**

Suppression of the truth to the prejudice of another. Bell. The expression is used by Hume, i., 137, to cover " a great variety of transgressions all . . . naturally reducible to the head of falsehood."

**Criminal letters.**

See *Letters.*

**Crop.**

See *Management, Clause of.*

**Credulity. Oath of**

An oath, as of verity (*q.v.*), except that it is made only to the best of the deponent's belief. See Bankruptcy Act, 1913, s. 22.

**Crown. Plea of the**

A criminal case triable only in the High Court of Justiciary. Such cases are murder, robbery, rape and fire-raising.

**Crown Agent.**

The chief Crown solicitor in criminal matters.

**Cruive.**

A wattled hedge built on tidal flats to catch fish. Chambers.

**Culreach.**

A person giving caution where an accused was demanded by one court of another. Obs.

**Culpable homicide.**

A killing caused by fault falling short of the evil intention required to constitute murder. It is like the English manslaughter.

**Curator.**

A person either entitled *ex lege* or appointed by the Court or an individual to administer the estate of another, as of a minor or insane person. Commonly mispronounced cúrator.

**Curator bonis.**

The person appointed to manage the estate of a minor in place of his legal guardian or to manage the estate of a person above minority suffering from mental or, less commonly, bodily infirmity. Irons, 247.

**Cursing. Letters of**

An ancient name for letters of excommunication.

**D**

**Daily Council.**

The Court, founded in 1503, which was the immediate predecessor of the Court of Session.

**Damnum fatale.**

A loss due to an unusual accident such as the occurrence of exceptional storm or flood.

**Dead's part of gear.**

The part of his moveables which a man has power to leave by will; one-third, one-half, or the whole according as he leaves wife and children, wife or children, or neither.

**Dean of Faculty.**

The elected leader of the Bar, whether of the Faculty of Advocates or of a local Bar of solicitors.

**Dean of Guild.**

A judge in certain burghs, formerly possessed of an important jurisdiction in mercantile disputes, now possessed of an important aedilic jurisdiction in the matter of building safety.

**Deathbed.**

The " law of deathbed " was a rule that the will of a testator in prejudice of his heir was bad if he died within sixty days of making it, of a disease affecting him when it was made, unless in the interval he had been seen at kirk or market. See *Ex capite lecti*.

**Debt.**

See *Document of Debt*.

**Debitum fundi.**

A debt secured over land, as for example, a feu-duty.

**Decern.**

An extremely formal verb meaning to give final decree or judgement, without the use of which the decree may not be extracted.

**Decimae.**
Teinds. When land is feued *cum decimis inclusis* it means that teind is not demandable by the person otherwise entitled to teind in that part ; *decimae rectoriae* or parsonage teinds were those formerly payable to the parson or rector and came from grain ; *decimae vicariae,* vicarage teinds or those paid to the vicar, came from such as wool, fish and eggs ; *decimae garbales,* the sheaves, one in every ten, which the rector of the parish was entitled to take.

**Declaration.**
The statement made in presence of the sheriff, and before he is committed, by a person whom it is intended to try on indictment Now rarely made.

**Declarator. Action of**
An action brought by an interested party to have some legal right declared but without claim on the defender to do anything.

**Declinature.**
Refusal to submit to a judge's jurisdiction on the score of interest or relationship.

**Decree.**
The common Scottish technical term for a final judgement. (The word as a term of art is accented on the first syllable.) Thus *decree arbitral,* the decision of an arbiter ; *decree conform,* a decree given by the Court of Session in aid of a lower court to enable diligence to be done ; *decree dative,* the judgement appointing a person executor. For *decree of locality,* of *modification,* of *registration* and of *valuation,* see under these words.

**Deed.**
A formal document, authenticated (except when holograph) by the maker's signature, the signatures of two witnesses, and a proper testing-clause.

**Defences.**
The statement by way of defence lodged by the defender in a civil action. The plural signifies, presumably, that the defender may rely on more legal answers than one. (In England this pleading is called the Defence.)

**Defender.**
The party against whom a civil action is brought.

**Deforcement.**
A crime consisting of resistance to officers of the law whilst executing their duty in civil matters.

### De fideli.

Short for *de fideli administratione*; the oath *de fideli administratione* is an oath taken by persons performing public duties that they will faithfully carry them out.

### Delectus personae.

Choice of a particular person. Important in a legal sense as preventing assignation or delegation of a duty by the person chosen.

### Delegation.

A form of novation which consists in the extinction of the liability of one party to a contract by the substitution of the liability of another. See Gloag on Contract, 258.

### Delict.

A wrong, nowadays always in a civil sense though formerly comprising crime too. Bell's Pr., 544.

### Deliverance.

A term used of the orders of the court in sequestrations. It is statutorily defined (Bankruptcy Act, 1913, s. 2) to include " any order, warrant, judgement, decision, interlocutor or decree." Originally more general in its application.

### Denude.

Of a trustee, to hand over the trust estate on giving up the office of trustee.

### Denunciation.

Denunciation as a rebel was the sequel to disobedience to a charge on *letters of horning* (*q.v.*).

### Deposit or Deposition.

A contract under which a moveable is entrusted by one (the depositor) to another (the depository or depositary) to be kept without reward.

### Depredation.

Forcible driving away of cattle. Obs.

### Dereliction.

Abandonment of something owned.

### Desert.

To *desert the diet* (the only particular use of this verb) is to give up a criminal charge, either *pro loco et tempore*, when a fresh charge can be brought or *simpliciter*, which is final.

### Design.

To set forth a person's occupation and address. Whence *designation*.

**Destination.**
A direction as to the persons who are to succeed to property. Used almost wholly of nomination by the owner, but see Bell, *sub voce*.

**Destination over.**
A destination to one person on failure of a precedent gift, usually by will, to another. As to its origin as an English term of art see *Hickling's Trs.* v. *Garland's Trs.* 1 F. (H.L.), 7.

**Devolution.**
See *Clause*.

**Devolve.**
Arbiters are said to devolve their decision to an oversman. Whence *devolution*.

**Dies cedit ; Dies venit.**
*Dies cedit* means that a right has vested in a person : *dies venit* means that it has become enforceable. See Connolly and Brown, *sub voce*.

**Diet.**
The date for hearing of a case for any one of a variety of purposes, fixed by the court. See *Desert*.

**Dilatory.**
Used of a defence, means one purely technical and not touching the merits.

**Diligence.**
Execution against debtors ; also a process for procuring the recovery of writings from an opponent or third party or for obtaining the evidence of witnesses before a commissioner.

**Disclamation.**
A casualty brought about through the disavowal of a superior by a vassal. Obs.

**Discuss.**
To proceed against one of two possible debtors, such as a principal debtor and a cautioner, as a preliminary to going against the other.

**Dispone.**
Of land, to convey. Formerly an essential word in any valid conveyance of land. Wood, 137.

**Disposition.**
A unilateral deed by which property heritable or moveable is alienated. Bell.

**Dispositive clause.**
The operative clause of a deed by which property is conveyed.

**Dittay.**

The matter of a criminal charge. To *take up dittay* was to obtain information and proof with a view to prosecution before Circuit Courts. Obs.

**Division. Action of**

An action by which common property is divided.

**Docquet.**

A summary of a longer writing. " The notarial docquet is the most ancient example of fixed style in Europe and it was formerly common to all solemn instruments. In Scotland it is almost exclusively appropriated to the instrument of sasine." Bell.

**Document of Debt.**

A document which constitutes evidence of a legal transaction or by which the indebtedness is created, *e.g.*, a bill of exchange. Loosely used.

**Dole.**

Evil intention, *malus animus*, malice in the legal sense. Adjective, *dolous*. Obsolescent, with *mens rea* gaining in favour as a substitute.

**Dominant tenement.**

A piece of land with the ownership of which goes a servitude right over adjoining land, the *servient* tenement.

**Dominium directum.**

The right in land enjoyed by the superior (*q.v.*).

**Dominium utile.**

The substantial right in land enjoyed by the vassal which would be known popularly as ownership.

**Dominus litis.**

The person really though not nominally behind legal proceedings, liable to be mulcted in expenses.

**Donatory.**

A person to whom property falling to the Crown, as by forfeiture, is given by the Crown.

**Doom.**

An ancient term for judgement or sentence, civil or criminal.

**Double distress.**

Two or more claims on a single fund, an essential of a *multiplepoinding* (*q.v.*).

**Double.**

A copy.

**Drawn teind.**

Grain taken as teind before removal of crop.

**Drove road.**
" The name given to a servitude road used for the passage of sheep or cattle to annual fairs or cattle markets." Bell.

**Dry multures.**
See *Multures.*

**Dyvour.**
Obsolete term for a bankrupt.

# E

**Eavesdrop.**
" The servitude of eavesdrop, or stillicide, imposes on the servient tenement the burden of receiving the drippings from the eaves of the dominant tenement." Bell.

**Edict.**
A writ formerly issued by the commissaries for citing those concerned upon the application of a person seeking to have executors appointed. Bell's Pr., 1894. Obs.

**Edictal citation.**
A mode of citing persons who are abroad ; formerly done by proclamation at Edinburgh and Leith, now by sending copies of the summons to the office of the Keeper of Edictal Citations.

**Effeirs. As**
Literally, as relates or corresponds ; duly, in the proper way, in due form.

**Effeiring to.**
Relating or appertaining to.

**Eik.**
An addition made to the inventory by an executor, so as to include additional property.

**Ejection.**
(i) Unlawful and violent casting out of a possessor from his heritage : leading to an *action of ejection* for its recovery. Stair, I., 9, 25. The action arises out of an ejection : it is not an action brought to secure ejection.
(ii) The putting out of a tenant by the landlord on the termination of his lease or when an irritancy is incurred.

**Elide.**
To oust or exclude.

**Embezzle.**
To turn to one's own use an article handed over for another purpose. The word has a different sense in English Law.

**Encumbrance.**
Usually means debt secured over land and thus encumbering it.

31

**Engrosser.**
See *Regrater.*

**Enorm.**
See *Lesion.*

**Entail.**
See *Tailzie.*

**Entry.**
Establishment of an heir, according to the rules of land tenure, as a new vassal with his superior.

**Equipollent.**
A legal synonym for equivalent.

**Erection. Lords of**
Persons to whom after the Reformation the Crown granted the land and the teinds formerly belonging to monasteries.

**Error. Summons of**
The initial step in a long disused process for setting aside an erroneous service of heirs.

**Escheat.**
Forfeiture of a man's estate. *Single escheat* is forfeiture of moveables to the Crown upon conviction of certain crimes of which murder is possibly to-day the only one. In the case of treason, escheat of all property is incurred. Formerly there was a feudal casualty of escheat, suffered through denunciation as a rebel for non-payment of debt and also through conviction of crime. It was for life only.

**Evidents.**
Writs and title-deeds, evidence of heritable rights. Practically obsolete.

**Examination.**
See *Declaration.*

*Ex capite lecti.*
Reduction of a will on the score of its being made on a man's deathbed in prejudice of his heir was called reduction *ex capite lecti* which appears to mean, literally, " reduction under the heading of bed " (*lectum*). See *Deathbed.*

**Exauctorated.**
Deprived of authority. Obs.

**Excambion.**
The contract under which one piece of land is exchanged for another.

**Exception.**
A defence. *Ope exceptionis*, by way of exception, is an expression also sometimes used. In both expressions the word seems to be used as simply meaning defence, without the implications of Roman Law.

**Exceptions. Bill of**
The mode of procedure by which legal objection to the verdict of a jury is brought under review by the Inner House of the Court of Session.

**Exchequer. Court of**
A court, now merged in the Court of Session, which was erected after the Union of 1707 upon the model of the English Court of Exchequer and charged particularly with the decision of Revenue questions.

**Exculpation. Letters of**
A warrant entitling an accused person to cite witnesses for his defence. Obs.

**Execution.**
The carrying out by an officer of the law of a citation or the like ; also the writing in which his fulfilment of the duty is narrated. Carrying out of a criminal sentence is also execution, but of a civil judgement is more usually styled diligence.

**Executor-creditor.**
A creditor who by way of diligence for recovery of his debt has himself confirmed as executor.

**Executor-dative.**
An executor appointed by the Court.

**Executor-nominate.**
An executor appointed by a testator.

**Executry.**
A comprehensive name for the whole moveable property of a person deceased.

***Ex parte.***
Proceedings are *ex parte* where the party against whom they are brought is not heard.

***Exercitor.***
A person (owner or charterer) who employs a ship in trade. Erskine, Pr. II., iii., 14. Practically obsolete.

**Exhibition. Action of**
An action to compel the delivery of writings to a party entitled, either *ad probandum* (*i.e.*, an accessory action, when not based on a right of property) in aid of a principal action, now largely obsolete ; or *ad deliberandum,* an action brought by an apparent heir to help him decide whether or not to take up the succession. See Maclaren, C.S.P., 644.

33

C

**Exoner.**
To discharge of liability. Thus a judicial factor may seek exoneration and discharge at the hands of the Court.

**Expede.**
To draw up, make out, complete, as of some instrument.

**Expenses.**
The Scottish technical expression for the costs of an action.

**Expose.**
Put up for sale by auction.

**Extent.**
(i) Valuation of land in Scotland. The *Old Extent* was made in the reign of Alexander III. (*c.* 1280) ; the New Extent dates from the Act 1474, c. 56.
(ii) *To extent* means, according to Jamieson, to assess ; from corrupt Latin use of *extendere*, whence also *stent*.

**Extract.**
A written instrument signed by the proper officer, containing a statement of a decree and if necessary, a warrant to charge the debtor and to execute all competent diligence against person or property. *To extract* is to procure this instrument.

**Extra-judicial.**
Bell defines as " Not transacted under judicial cognisance or superintendence." The word to-day occurs perhaps most often in the expression *extra-judicial expenses*, meaning expenses not recoverable from the other side.

**Extrinsic.**
When on a reference to his oath a party makes an admission but subject to an explanation, the explanation is *extrinsic* or *intrinsic*, according as it is considered separable or inseparable from what is sworn : the latter qualifies the oath, the former does not. Lewis on Evidence, 153.

## F

**Facility and circumvention.**
When one person by a dishonest course of conduct plays upon a facile person in order to secure an advantage there is *facility and circumvention*.

**Factor.**
According to Bell (Comm. I., 507), a factor is one who with possession of goods buys or sells on commission for a principal. He differs from an agent in that his authority extends to the management of all the principal's affairs in the place where he lives. But in Scotland this precise meaning of the word is not now usual. See *Judicial Factor*.

34

**Factory.**
A deed granted by A empowering B to act for him in one or several transactions. Wood, 675. The English *Power of Attorney* seems to be displacing the Scots term.

**Factum praestandum.**
An obligation *ad factum praestandum* is an obligation to do or perform some act other than the payment of money. Erskine, Pr. III., iv., 25.

**Faculty.**
A power which may be exercised at any time.

**Falsehood, fraud, and wilful imposition.**
The *nomen juris* of the crime which consists, substantially, in obtaining by false pretences.

**Falsing of doom.**
Ancient term for the reversing of decrees. See, *e.g.*, Hume, ii., 6.

**Fama clamosa.**
A report current as to a minister's or elder's immorality.

**Fatuous.**
Imbecile and incapable of managing one's own affairs. Also used as a noun. Practically obsolete.

**Feal and divot.**
The name of a servitude giving a right of cutting turf, for which *feal* and *divot* are Scots equivalents.

**Fee.**
The full right of property in heritage, as contradistinguished from liferent.

**Fee-fund.**
The account or fund in the Court of Session into which court dues are paid, and which is used to pay salaries of officials of the Court.

**Feriat days.**
*Dies non.* Obs.

**Feu.**
A feudal holding. *To feu* is, strictly, to give out land upon a feudal arrangement whereby the vassal (buyer) holds land of a superior (the landowner) usually upon the terms that he builds on the land and pays a perpetual rent, or *feu duty*. He is virtually owner so long as he pays and observes any conditions. A piece of land thus feued is sometimes referred to as a *feu*.

**Fiar.**
The owner of a fee.

**Fiars.**
The average prices of grain fixed annually at the Fiars Court for determination of minister's stipends. The word is apparently akin to *fier* or *feer*, a standard of any kind. Jamieson.

**Filiation.**
The determination by a court of the paternity of a child, usually a bastard.

**Fire and sword. Letters of**
An obsolete remedy given by the Privy Council to enforce decrees of removing.

**Fire-raising.**
The Scottish technical term for arson.

**Firm.**
Besides its meaning of a partnership, this word also means the partnership- or firm-name.

**Fiscal.**
See *Procurator Fiscal*.

**Fitted accounts.**
Accounts between parties who have had business transactions, rendered by one and docqueted as correct by the other without any formal discharge. This puts the onus of proving that some account is still outstanding upon the person so claiming. Gloag on Contract, p. 723.

**Force and fear.**
The Scottish technical term for duress, vitiating a contract.

**Forehand rent.**
Rent payable by agreement in advance of the legal term of payment.

**Forestall.**
To buy something which is on the way to market or to dissuade one from taking it there, or to do something to enhance the price in the market. Formerly a crime. See Hume, i., 510, and cf. *Regrate*.

**Forethought felony.**
Seems to have been equivalent to malice or evil intention. Obs.

**Forisfamiliation.**
The departure of a child from the family on setting-up on his or her own account or marrying.

**Forthcoming.**
An action which the arrester of property must bring against arrestee and common debtor in order to make the arrested property available or " forthcoming." Often, *furthcoming*.

**Fossa.**
A pit, used anciently for drowning a thief. See *Furca*.

**Fructus : fruits.**
As a legal term includes fruit proper and also grain. *Fructus pendentes* are fruits not gathered. *Fructus percepti*, fruits which have been gathered.

**Fugitation.**
Outlawry for failing to appear to answer to a criminal charge. The verb to *fugitate* is also known.

**Fund** *in medio.*
See *Multiplepoinding*.

**Fungible.**
Fungibles are goods meant for consumption.

**Furca.**
A fork-shaped gallows. Grants of jurisdiction were sometimes *cum furca et fossa (q.v.).*

**Furiosity.**
Insanity. The term is practically obsolete, as is the adjective *furious*.

**Furthcoming.**
See *Forthcoming*.

**Furtum grave.**
A theft so serious as formerly to warrant the death penalty. See Hume, i., 91.

**Furth of.**
Outside the borders of.

## G

**Gable.**
See *Mutual Gable*.

**General Assembly.**
The highest church court in Scotland.

**General charge.**
A charge, of 40 days, directed to the heir of a deceased owner of land commanding him to have himself established as heir to the deceased. This was followed by *special* or *general special charge (q.v.).* See further, Duff, pp. 302–3, and see *Charge, supra*.

**General disposition.**
A deed meant as a conveyance but lacking the pre-requisites of infeftment, *e.g.*, a proper description of the land. Wood, 302.

**General service.**
See *Service*.

### Gestio pro haerede.
Occurs when a person behaves as though he were heir, thereby incurring liability for debt up to the value of the estate to which he succeeds.

### Gift.
In addition to its normal lay sense and its more technical use as meaning a bequest, this word has had the meaning of a grant by the Crown, as, *e.g.*, in a *gift of tutory*, where the Exchequer appointed tutors. See Bell for examples.

### Girth and sanctuary.
Girth and sanctuary are, *semble*, synonyms (see Jamieson, *sub voce* girth). The phrase indicates the protection given to one who after killing without malice aforethought reached sanctuary. Obs.

### Glebe.
Land to the use of which a minister in a landward parish has a right, over and above his stipend. Erskine, Pr. I., v., 16.

### Goods in Communion.
Moveable property formerly belonging in common to husband and wife. Bell.

### Gowpen.
See *Lock*.

### Grace. Act of
See *Act of Grace*.

### Grana crescentia.
A thirlage (as to which see under *Sucken*) was of *omnia grana crescentia* when it applied to all corn grown upon the ground in question.

### Grant.
The word denotes an original disposition and also a gratuitous deed. There is a helpful note on this word in Bell.

### Grassum.
A single payment made in addition to a periodic payment such as rent or feu-duty. Despite its appearance the word is of A.S. origin, being a form of *gersum*. Murray calls it a premium paid to a feudal superior and cites English use in that sense, but in England it is obsolete.

### Gratuitous.
Made or granted without consideration.

### Great avizandum.
A report by the Lord Ordinary to the Inner House in certain actions, such as proving the tenor, in order that judgement might be given. Largely obsolete.

**Ground-annual.**
An annual payment for land stipulated for when land was given off ior building and subinfeudation was prohibited, the liability for it forming a real burden (*q.v.*) on the land and the relationship between the creditor and debtor not being a feudal one. The ground-annual was also used in the case of church lands. See Bell's Pr., 885–8.

**Grounds and warrants.**
An expression used in an action of restriction of a decree, meaning the reasons and the documentary evidence upon which the decree was based and which may be called for in the action. Shand's Pract., ii., 635, 719.

# H

**Habile.**
Apt, or competent for some purpose.

**Habit and repute.**
In the law of theft, means the reputation of being a thief, the words being used in aggravation of the particular charge. In civil law it is the reputation of being married which, coupled with cohabitation, constitutes an irregular marriage.

*Haereditas iacens.*
An estate of inheritance not taken up by the heir.

**Hamesucken.**
An assault committed upon a man in his own house.

**Hasp and staple.**
The clasp and hoop, to which a padlock is attached for fastening a door ; used symbolically in entering (*q.v.*) an heir in burgage property. The words are English usage in a lay sense.

**Haver.**
A person having documents in his possession which he is required to produce as evidence in a lawsuit. Pronounced hăvver.

**Hearing in presence.**
See *Presence. Hearing in*

**Heir.**
The person who succeeds to the property of a person deceased, whether by force of law or by express provision, and whether the property is heritable or moveable, although the word is felt to be much more appropriate as applied to heritage. Its meaning is lent greater precision by appending other words, thus : *heir-apparent*, strictly an English expression meaning one who is bound to succeed X if only he survive him, with which contrast *apparent heir, supra* : *heir-at-law*, the person

39

succeeding by force of law, also known as *heir-general, heir whatsoever,* and *heir of line* (Erskine, Pr. III., viii., 4) ; *heir-female,* one of either sex who succeeds though a female ; *heir-male,* the nearest heir who is a male and who is related solely through males ; *heir-presumptive,* one who is nearest heir at a given moment but whose right may be ousted by the birth of a nearer ; *heir of provision,* one who succeeds in virtue of express provisions as in a settlement ; *heir of entail,* one entitled to succeed to entailed lands, so called, too, even after succeeding ; *heirs-portioners,* women succeeding to heritage jointly as heirs-portioners (but any one predeceasing will be represented by her heir as heir-portioner, even if he is a male) ; *heirs in mobilibus,* those entitled to succeed to moveables, including therein, not only the next-of-kin but their representatives, now by statute admitted to the succession.

## Heirship moveables.

There was a right in the heir, now abolished, to take certain moveables so that he should not receive his property wholly bare ; these were heirship moveables.

## Herezeld.

Synonymous with the Scots and English term *heriot,* meaning the best beast belonging to a tenant which the landlord could claim on the tenant's death.

## Heritage.

The technical term for property in the form of land and houses, because it passed to the heir on the owner's death. Whence the epithet *heritable,* as in *heritable securities* (*e.g.,* heritable bonds), sums of money secured to the creditor over land ; *heritable jurisdictions,* rights of judicature which passed with land and which are now abolished.

## Heritor.

Strictly, any landowner, but in practice confined to a landowner in his rôle of a person liable to contribute to the upkeep of the parish church.

## Hership or herdship.

Another term for *depredation, q.v.* Obs.

## High Constable.

See *Constable.*

## High Court.

See *Justiciary.*

## Hinc inde.

A good Latin phrase used frequently with such words as " claims," meaning the claims made on one side and on the other.

**Holding.**
Tenure in a feudal sense, as in blench-holding, ward-holding, feu-holding, and others.

**Holograph.**
Wholly written by one person. See *Probative.*

**Homagium.**
A bond of *manrent, q.v.*

**Homologate.**
To approve, and so validate, as of a defective contract.

**Horning.**
A highly penal diligence for debt. A creditor obtained *letters of horning* directing officers of the law to *charge* the debtor to pay : if the latter failed, the officer blew three blasts with a horn at the appropriate market-cross and then published the fact, which constituted *denunciation at the horn.* The defender became a rebel and was subject to *single escheat, i.e.,* forfeiture of his moveables to the Crown. See Erskine, Pr. II., v. 23.

**Hypothec.**
A right in security over effects of a debtor, valid without possession by the creditor : *e.g.,* hypothec for rent and feu-duty and maritime hypothec.

## I

**Idiot.**
See *Fatuous.*

**Illiquid.**
The opposite of *liquid, q.v.*

**Immemorial.**
In its legal sense the word, though vague, means something much less than in the ordinary sense. See Bell.

**Impignoration.**
Pledging or pawning.

**Improbation.**
A proving false or forged, as by the action of improbation.

**Improbatory articles.**
See *Articles, Improbatory and Approbatory.*

**Improbative.**
Not *probative, q.v.*

**Improving lease.**
A lease of abnormal duration granted to encourage the tenant to improve a dilapidated farm. Bell.

**Incendiary letter.**
A threatening letter.

### Incident diligence.
Diligence, formerly obtained by a substantive action, and then later in course of an existing action, by which havers were compelled to produce writs. See Stair, IV., xxxiii., 3. The phrase is obsolete, although of course the thing itself is a commonplace of practice.

### Incompetent.
An action is incompetent when the conclusions (*i.e.*, the demand for a remedy) conflict with a rule of law applicable in the circumstances. See *Irrelevant*. Maclaren, C.S.P., 3 and 7–8.

### Indictment.
An accusation of crime running in the name of the Lord Advocate, tried by a jury in serious cases in the High Court or Sheriff Court. See *Major proposition*.

### *Induciae.*
The period allowed for his appearance to a person served with legal process. (Latin, *indutiae*, a pause.) Commonly treated as a singular noun.

### Industrial.
Brought about by the industry of a man as, *e.g.*, industrial crops, which means crops sown by man, not growing wild.

### Infamy.
When a person was convicted of perjury or the like, this was *infamia juris*, or that infamy which disqualified a man as a witness.

### Infangthef.
"The right to judge and punish a thief caught with the fang (the booty) within the grantee's jurisdiction." Cosmo Innes, 57. *Outfangthef* gave power over one similarly caught outside the jurisdiction.

### Infeftment.
The symbolical act, now obsolete, of putting a man into possession of heritage and so completing his title. As a result he was *infeft*.

### Infer.
To involve as a consequence. In lay usage only a person infers, but in legal usage such and such a course of conduct, for example, infers a penalty.

### Information.
A written argument ordered by the Lord Ordinary in reporting a case to the Inner House. Later called a *Case*. Both now obsolete. Bell.

**Ingather.**
To collect or get in money or property due ; used of executors, trustees, and the like.

**Inhibition.**
A writ which prohibits a debtor from burdening his heritage or parting with it to the detriment of the inhibiting creditor.

***In hoc statu.***
In this state of matters ; at this stage.

***In initialibus.***
The examination *in initialibus*, at one time held, was to determine the admissibility of a witness.

***In litem.***
The oath *in litem* was that of the pursuer, swearing to value. in an action of delict based on the loss or destruction of goods. It constituted proof without corroboration. Dickson, s. 1514. Obs.

**Inner House.**
The two appellate divisions of the Court of Session, so-called originally on the simple topographical ground that their Court lay further from the entrance to the Courthouse than did the Outer House. See Hannay, College of Justice, 95.

**Innominate contract.**
A contract not falling within one of the well-known and named classes of contracts, which if also *unusual* requires to be proved by writing.

**Innovation.**
See *Novation*.

**Inquest.**
A body, part jury part witness, which made inquiry into such matters as the service of heirs and cognition of the insane. Stair, III., 5, 30.

***In rem suam.***
An adverbial phrase meaning to one's own advantage.

***In rem versum.***
An adjectival phrase meaning turned to one's own account.

***In retentis.***
Literally, amongst things kept for record : evidence is taken to lie *in retentis* when taken before the regular hearing of a case, where otherwise there is a risk of its being lost.

***In solidum.***
For the whole sum.

*Institor.*

A term of Roman Law sometimes but now rarely used in Scots Law as meaning an agent or manager. Erskine, Pr. III., iii., 14 (46).

**Institute.**

The person first named or called in a destination of property ; those who follow upon him are *substitutes*. A *conditional institute* is one substituted to the institute in such terms that if the institute survive the granter he, the conditional institute, can never take. In this he is unlike the substitute.

**Instruct.**

To vouch or support, used of a thing not a person.

**Instrument.**

A document, usually under the seal of a notary, testifying to the completion of such juristic acts as sasine and assignation. *To take instruments* is to make some sort of formal protest, the exact nature of which is not very clear. See Jamieson, *sub voce.*

**Intercommuning. Letters of**

" Letters " from the Scots Privy Council prohibiting the public from holding intercourse with named persons guilty of crime. Bell. Obs.

**Interdict.**

The judicial prohibition issued by a Scottish Court, comparable with the English injunction. In an emergency *interim interdict* can be obtained on application *ex parte.*

**Interdiction.**

A mode whereby a weak-minded person restrains himself by bond from affecting his heritage without the consent of certain persons styled *interdictors.*

**Interim.**

See *Interdict.*

**Interlocutor.**

Strictly, an order or decision of the Court short of the final judgement, but in practice applied to any order of the Court. *Interlocutor sheets* are a document, part of a process, on which the Court's interlocutors are entered.

**Intermeddle.**

To interfere improperly or without any right.

**Interrogatories.**

Written questions adjusted by the Court, to be put to witnesses examined under a commission.

**Interruption.**

The word is used of certain acts which frustrate the running of a period of prescription.

44

**Intimation. Letters of**
Notification to the Lord Advocate that he is required to bring a prisoner to trial under the Act of 1701. Obs.

**Intrinsic.**
See *Extrinsic.*

**Inter vivos.**
Between living persons : used of deeds meant to take effect during the granter's life as distinguished from deeds *mortis causa,* which only take effect on death.

**Intromit with.**
To handle or deal with, as funds or other property : whence *intromission ; intromitter.* See *Vitious intromission.*

**Intrusion.**
The entering on possession of heritable property without violence but without any right.

**Invade.**
To invade a judge was *semble,* to assault him. Stair, IV. 36, 6, mentions *Invasion.* See Hume, i., 405.

**Invecta et illata.**
Effects brought onto premises, usually the effects of a tenant. The words appear to be pure synonyms.

**Inventory.**
A list of the moveable property of a person deceased, which must be sworn to and lodged by executors on taking up their duties.

**Inventory. With benefit of**
When an heir made and recorded an inventory of the heritage to which he succeeded, he was liable only to the extent of the estate for the obligations of his predecessor.

**Inventory of process.**
An inventory of the documents in a process which must be lodged in court along with them. So, too, there is an *inventory of productions.*

**Investiture.**
The progress or series of titles, by which a real right in lands is vested in the proprietor.

**Impetrate.**
Procure, obtain ; as a rule pejorative in its implication.

**Irritancy.**
The forfeiture of a right in consequence of neglect or contravention. Bell. It may be *legal* (implied by law) or *conventional* (the result of agreement).

**Irritant and resolutive.**
See *Clause.*

**Irritate.**
To enforce the right of forfeiture. Presumably from Latin *irritus,* invalid.

**Implement.**
To fulfil or carry out, as of duty, promise or contract.

**Irregular marriage.**
A marriage perfectly valid but carried through without the intervention of ecclesiastical or civil authority ; to-day, only by cohabitation with habit and repute, but formerly by interchange of consent and by promise followed by intercourse (*subsequente copula*). See Gloag and Henderson, 4th Ed., 572.

**Irrelevant.**
The opposite of *relevant, q.v.*

**Ish.**
Termination (issue), commonly of a lease.

**Issue.**
The formal question put for decision to a jury in a civil case.

*Iter.*
A servitude allowing one to pass over the land of another.

## J

**Jedge and warrant.**
An authority given by the Dean of Guild to repair or rebuild ruinous houses and to constitute the expense a real burden on the property.

**Joint adventure.**
A partnership for one particular transaction.

**Joint obligation.**
An obligation binding several, yet each only for a share. The English legal use is different.

**Jointure.**
A provision in favour of a wife, against her widowhood, consisting, according to Bell, Comm. I., 682, of an annuity secured upon heritage. An English term, but used in Scotland as early as Bankton (ii., 289).

**Judge Ordinary.**
" A judge whether supreme or inferior who by the nature of his office has a fixed and determinate jurisdiction in all actions of the same general nature." Bell.

*Judicatum solvi.*
Caution *judicatum solvi* is an undertaking that a sum of money found due by the court will be paid.

**Judicial factor.**
A person appointed by the Court to manage property of someone who for one of a number of reasons, such as minority, defective intellect, absence from the country and others, is not able to manage it for himself.

**Judicial reference.**
A reference of a matter to arbitration under authority of the Court. Bell.

**Judicial sale.**
A sale under the authority of the Court in various circumstances, as for example of poinded effects, or of property comprised in a heritable security.

*Judicio sisti.*
An undertaking *judicio sisti* is an undertaking to appear in Court to answer a claim.

**Juratory caution.**
This is inadequate caution allowed in some cases where the party swears that he cannot find other or better caution. See Mackay's Manual, 430.

*Jus administrationis.*
The right as of a curator formerly enjoyed by a husband, in respect of his wife's heritage. Abolished.

*Jus crediti.*
A right vested in a creditor, not necessarily of instant payment.

*Jus deliberandi.*
The right of an heir to six months (formerly a year) in which to decide whether or not to avail himself of his right to succeed.

*Jus devolutum.*
A right which has for lack of exercise devolved on another. Used in ecclesiastical law of the right to appoint a minister, devolving on the presbytery when the congregation fails to appoint.

*Jus ad rem.*
A right to claim a thing from the debtor in an obligation (it is thus also a *jus in personam*) but not to claim it as against all the world which is *jus in re* and is really a right of property.

*Jus mariti.*
The right of the husband, now abolished, to the property in the wife's moveables, except *paraphernalia, q.v.* (Stress the second syllable of *mariti.*)

*Jus preventionis.*
An expression of little practical account and seldom used, meaning the alleged preferable right of a Court which is seised of a case before another or others equally competent.

**Jus in personam.**
See *Jus ad rem.*

**Jus in re.**
See *Jus ad rem.*

**Jus quaesitum tertio.**
A contractual right of one party, A, arising out of a contract between X and Y, to which A is not a party.

**Jus relictae.**
The widow's right to one-third or one-half of her deceased husband's moveable property, according as there are or are not children.

**Jus relicti.**
The widower's right comparable to *jus relictae.*

**Jus tertii.**
A third party's right ; the expression is used when one denies that A has any such right as he alleges, though it might properly enough be claimed by X, a third party.

**Justice Ayres.**
An archaic expression for the circuits followed by the judges of the Justiciary Court.

**Justice-Clerk. Lord**
The second in dignity of the Scottish judges, who presides over the second Division of the Court of Session. The title, like that of the Master of the Rolls, points to his comparatively humble beginnings as a Clerk of Court.

**Justice. College of**
See *College of Justice.*

**Justice-General. Lord**
See *Justiciar.*

**Justiciar.**
The ancient name, now obsolete, for the highest criminal judge in Scotland. The modern title is Lord Justice-General.

**Justiciary. High Court of**
The supreme Criminal Court of Scotland, consisting of thirteen judges (Lords Commissioners of Justiciary) who are also the thirteen judges of the Court of Session.

**Justifiable homicide.**
Killing in exercise of a public duty as, *e.g.*, execution of sentence of death, or of a private right, as, *e.g.*, of self-defence.

## K

**Kain (also Cane).**
Animals or fowls, paid in lieu of feu-duty or rent.

**Kenning to terce.**
The procedure whereby the sheriff fixed the lands falling under the widow's terce. Now abolished.

**Kindly tenant or rentaller.**
A holder of land who, without having a feudal relationship with a superior, came to have what Bell calls " a sort of hereditary right." Writers vary in their accounts of the kindly tenant. See Bell's Pr., 1279–82.

**King's and Lord Treasurer's Remembrancer.**
The general administrator of the Crown revenues in Scotland. See the short article in Bell's Dictionary for a historical account.

**King's Keys.**
See *Open doors. Letters of.*

**King's freemen.**
Persons who because of service in the Army and Navy had a right to exercise a trade as freemen without becoming members of the corporation of their trade. Bell.

**Kirk or market.**
See *Deathbed.*

**Kirk-Session.**
The church court which consists of the minister and elders of a parish.

**Knaveship.**
A quantity of grain paid to the miller's servant for work done at the mill.

<h2 style="text-align:center">L</h2>

*Labes realis.*
An inherent taint or defect in a title to property, such for instance as affects stolen goods. Sometimes called *vitium reale.*

*Labores.*
Lands cultivated by monks which were teind free.

**Lady's gown.**
Presents formerly made to a married woman on the sale of lands with her consent and forming a *peculium, q.v.* Bell's Pr., 1560.

**Lammas.**
The first of August.

**Land tax.**
Tax on land in Scotland, fixed at the date of the Union at £47,954 per annum. Now paid solely in counties. See *Extent.*

**Last heir.**
See *Ultimus haeres.*

D

**Law agent.**

A common term (often shortened to " agent ") for a solicitor or writer. The expression found statutory sanction in a number of Acts (*e.g.*, the Law Agents' Act, 1873), but the tendency to-day is to substitute the English term " solicitor." See for example the Solicitors (Scotland) Act, 1933.

**Law burrows.**

Caution or security, to the intent that the person bound will keep the peace towards the complainer and his family. *Burgh* or *burrow* anciently meant a cautioner.

**Lead.**

To lead evidence is to adduce or call evidence. The expression to " lead proof " is also used.

**Leasing-making.**

Slander of the King or Prince of Scotland or his Council. Obs.

**Leasum.**

Archaic word for lawful.

**Legal.**

In addition to being used as an adjective, this word is used as a noun, meaning the period allowed by the law to a person whose property is in course of being adjudged, within which he may pay the debt and free the land of the adjudication. When *declarator of expiry of the legal* is pronounced the right to redeem is irretrievably lost.

**Legitim.**

See *Bairns' part of gear.*

**Legitimation** *per subsequens matrimonium.*

The rendering legitimate of a bastard by the subsequent marriage of his parents.

*Lenocinium.*

Furtherance by a husband of adultery committed by his wife. It constitutes a defence to an action of divorce by a husband.

*Leonina societas.*

A partnership in which one partner takes all the gain, the other bears all the loss.

**Lesion.**

Detriment, loss, or injury. When *enorm*, or considerable, a minor suffering it may have a transaction which is to his lesion set aside on the ground of *minority and lesion.*

**Letters.**

A writ or warrant issued by the court and under the signet. Procedure for a great variety of purposes was inaugurated by letters, but their use is now practically obsolete. Thus there were *letters of advocation, exculpation, caption, horning, inhibition, intercommuning, open doors,* and *relaxation,* for which, see these various words. Others were *letters conform,* as to which see *decree conform: criminal letters,* a form of criminal charge in which, differing from indictment, the general style is a command of the King to answer the charge set out ; *letters of four forms,* the first step in execution against the person, consisting of four charges, the last being to the debtor to enter prison on pain of denunciation, *q.v.* ; *letters of slains,* acknowledgment by the wife or executor of a person killed by another that they had received satisfaction. Erskine, Pr. IV., 4, 64.

### Lex loci contractus.
The law of the place where a contract was made, which is often the proper law by which to decide disputes about contracts.

### Libel.
In addition to its meaning of written defamation, this word also has the meaning of a criminal indictment. The verb *to libel* also bears both meanings, to defame in writing and to charge as a crime.

### Lick thumbs.
Licking thumbs was an act in ancient times symbolic of the conclusion of a bargain.

### Liege poustie.
The state of health which prevented challenge of a will under the law of deathbed. From Latin, *legitima potestas.*

### Liege.
A subject of the King.

### Lien.
The right to retain the property of a debtor until he pays. An English term now widely used in Scotland : it is dissyllabic. See *Retention.*

### Liferent.
Strictly, a personal servitude, which entitles a man to the use for his life of another's property, though the liferenter's right is rather that of an owner for life. It is a *proper liferent* when only fiar and liferenter are involved : *improper liferent* when trustees are interposed : it is *legal* when imposed by law (*e.g.,* terce), *conventional* when agreed ; it is by *reservation* when the granter gives the fee but keeps a liferent, by *constitution* when he creates the liferent for another and keeps or disposes elsewhere of the fee.

### Light.
A servitude binding one owner of property not to build or plant on it so as to obstruct the light of his neighbour.

**Lining.**
Strictly the fixing or marking out of the boundaries of land. Commonly used in a wider sense to mean a *decree of lining*, i.e. the order of a Dean of Guild, authorising the erection or alteration of a building.

**Liquid.**
Of fixed and ascertained amount. A liquid debt is one ascertained and constituted against a debtor by written obligation or by judgement of a court. *Liquidate damages* means a sum of damages ascertained in advance inserted in a contract and exigible on a breach of the contract.

**Litigious.**
When land is rendered litigious it cannot be alienated so as to disappoint creditors. This condition is brought about by registration of a summons for reducing a title to the land or attaching it for debt. *Litigiosity* then exists. See Erskine, Pr. II., xi, 8a.

**Litiscontestation.**
Joinder of issue. In modern Scots law it arises on the lodging of defences.

**Locality.**
A Teind Court decree, delimiting the amount of minister's stipend for which each heritor (*q.v.*) is responsible. Bell. Also an appropriation of lands to a wife in liferent by provision in her marriage-contract. Bell's Pr., 1947. Obsolete in this sense.

**Location.**
Hire, whether of a person's services or of premises. The term is obsolescent.

**Lock.**
A small quantity ; used of the small quantity of meal given to the servant of a mill. The word *gowpen*, the hands held together like a concave measure, was used in the same sense. Jamieson.

**Lockfast place.**
A room, cupboard, box, and the like within a house, the breaking into which constitutes an aggravation of theft.

*Locus.*
The Latin word for place, beloved of the police and certain lawyers in referring to the spot where an event of importance for the matter in hand has taken place.

*Locus poenitentiae.*
The opportunity to withdraw from a contract which is not binding on account of its informality : it is ousted by some form of personal bar as, *e.g.*, *rei interventus*.

**Locus standi.**
The right to be heard before a tribunal. Usually of the right to appear before a Parliamentary Committee in opposition to a private bill.

**Lodge.**
To lodge pleadings and other documents is to leave them in the custody of the Clerk of Court. The English lawyer uses *file*.

**Loose.**
To remove, cancel, or take off, as, *e.g.*, an arrestment.

**Lord.**
For this word in conjunction with others as in *Lord President, Lord High Admiral*, see *passim*, under the latter part of the title.

**Lovite.**
A formally affectionate term for a subject of the King when addressed or referred to in certain formal documents. It was formerly a word of style descriptive of the pursuer in a Court of Session summons.

**Lucrative succession.**
Before an heir incurred liability through *praeceptio hereditatis* (*q.v.*), it had to be shewn that he had received the grant by a lucrative succession, *i.e.*, that it was pure gain to him and that he had given no consideration.

**Lyon King of Arms. Lord**
The principal administrative officer, who is also a judge, in Scottish heraldic matters.

## M

**Macers.**
Mace-bearers or ushers in the Court of Session: they had formerly more important functions than at the present time. Bell.

**Magistrate.**
The usual meaning is the provost or a bailie of a town. The word is scarcely if at all used in Scotland as in England of justices of the peace.

**Mail or maill.**
An obsolete word for rent, as in *grass mail*, the grazing rent for cattle. But it survives in the expression, *maills and duties*, an action of *maills and duties* being a form of diligence by which a heritable creditor procures the rents of the property to be paid direct to him.

**Major.**
A person of full legal age, *i.e.*, 21.

**Major proposition.**
That part of the old form of indictment (which was in the form of a syllogism) which named or described the crime of which in the minor proposition the accused person was, circumstantially, stated to be guilty.

**Mala fide possessor.**
One who possesses property upon a title which he knows or should know to be bad.

**Male appretiata.**
Wrongly valued ; applied to the property of a deceased person, where a wrong valuation calls for a corrective inventory.

**Malicious mischief.**
Damage done to property out of malice or cruelty.

**Man of skill.**
The technical name for an expert in some particular subject to whom a remit may be made by a Court for his report on some question arising in the case.

**Mandate.**
An authority given by one man to act (and strictly, to act gratuitously) for another.

**Manrent.**
A kind of bondage under which free-men passed *in clientelam* of their patrons. Now abolished.

**Manse.**
The dwelling provided for a parish minister.

**March.**
Boundary ; although common to both Scots and English this word is used with special frequency by Scots lawyers.

**Marischal.**
An officer of state who as judge, had jurisdiction in the case of crimes committed within a certain distance of his itinerant court. Pronounced marshall. Obs.

**Mark or merk.**
An old Scottish silver coin, worth about 1s. 2d. sterling.

**Marriage.**
The name of a casualty entitling the superior to a payment on the marriage of the vassal's heir.

**Marriage-contract.**
A contract entered into *ante-* or *post-nuptially* between persons about to be or actually married, for the purpose of regulating the rights in property of themselves and their children. Sometimes called a *marriage-settlement*, the English expression.

**Martinmas.**

A term-day in Scotland, the 11th of November. By virtue of the Act 49 and 50 Vict. c. 50, the actual Martinmas removals take place on 28th November.

***Meditatione fugae* warrant.**

When a debtor is contemplating flight abroad, he may be apprehended and imprisoned in a limited number of cases on a *meditatione fugae warrant.* It is rarely granted.

***Medium concludendi.***

A ground of action.

**Meliorations.**

The technical expression for improvements to property made by such as a tenant or liferenter. Not much used.

**Merchant.**

In old Scots usage, a shopkeeper : cf. the expression *merchand's compts* in the Act 1579, c. 83.

**Merk.**

See *Mark, supra.*

**Messengers-at-Arms.**

Formerly called Officers-at-Arms, are officers appointed by the Lord Lyon King of Arms, whose function is to execute civil and criminal process of the Court of Session and High Court of Justiciary : so-called by reason of the *blazon* (*q.v.*) which they wear.

**Messuage.**

In Scottish usage means the principal dwelling-house of a barony. Bell. ·

**Mid-couples.**

The documents of title by which a person taking infeftment in virtue of a *precept of sasine* (*q.v.*), granted to his predecessor, shewed how he came to have a right to avail himself of the precept.

**Mid-impediment.**

An event occurring between two others which prevents the later from operating retrospectively upon the earlier. Was most commonly used in the unreformed law of conveyancing.

**Minor.**

By this is usually meant a young person, between 12 and 21, if female ; 14 and 21, if male. But it may be used in the wider sense of a person under 21.

**Minor proposition.**

See *Major proposition.*

**Minority and lesion.**

See *Lesion.*

**Minute.**
A document forming part of a process by means of which a party (or parties, jointly) defines his position as to certain procedural matters as, *e.g.*, by amending his pleadings, by referring to the oath of his adversary or by abandoning the action.

**Minute-book.**
A book kept in the Register of Sasines in which are entered details, names of parties, date of presentation, etc., of deeds presented for registration.

**Minute-book (of Court of Session).**
" A book in which are minuted or shortly stated, the heads of the judgements, that is of the acts and decrees pronounced by the Court or by Lords Ordinary," *i.e.*, in the Court of Session. Bell.

**Missives.**
Informal and preliminary writings exchanged, though not necessarily sent, by parties negotiating for a contract, which may or may not be binding according as the nature of the contract in view does not or does demand formal writing.

**Mobbing.**
The combination against peace and good order for an illegal purpose of an assemblage of people.

**Modify.**
To reduce below the competent maximum, as expenses or a penalty.

**Modification.**
A Teind Court decree granting a certain stipend to a minister out of the teinds of the parish, but without proportioning it out amongst the heritors. Erskine, Pr. I., v., 13. See *Locality*.

*Modus.*
(*a*) The narration of the facts and circumstances in a criminal charge.
(*b*) Teind when valued is said to be paid by a modus. Bell.

**Molestation. Action of**
An action for defence of the possession of heritage against molestation or the troubling of the pursuer in his possession. Obs.

*Mora.*
The delay in asserting a claim, which, when coupled with prejudice to the defender, may prevent the pursuer from recovering.

**Mortancestry. Brieve of**
A brieve issued in the case where an heir was excluded from the land by the superior or other claimant who was therefore made party to the suit. Erskine, Pr. III., viii., 28. See *Brieve*.

**Mortification.**
The granting of land to a perpetual owner, *i.e.*, *ad manum mortuam*, to a dead hand—dead because it could not pass on the property to another, or because, the owner being immortal, no casualties were exigible. See Erskine, Pr. II., iv., 5.

*Mortis causa.*
On account of death : an instrument is made *mortis causa* when it is intended to take effect after death.

**Motion.**
An application made in Court for some subsidiary purpose during the course of an action.

**Mournings.**
Mourning clothes, to which a widow has a legal right out of her husband's estate, upon his death.

**Moveables.**
All property other than heritage. The reason for assigning property to one class or other is usually but not always obvious ; see Erskine, Pr. II., ii., 1.

**Muirburn.**
The seasonal burning of heather which, with due care, a proprietor has a right to carry out.

**Multiplepoinding.**
An action brought, actually or nominally, by a person who holds property, styled the *fund in medio*, upon which conflicting claims (*double distress*) are made, in order that the Court may decide who is entitled to it. See *Nominal raiser.*

**Multures.**
The grain which had to be given to the miller of a particular mill, to which the owners or tenants of land were sometimes *astricted* or *thirled*, in return for his grinding the rest. *Insucken multures* (see *sucken*) came from those astricted ; *outsucken* from those not astricted. By *dry multures* is meant duties paid in money or grain, whether grain was ground or not. Where the grain was taken elsewhere in fraud of the mill, an action for *abstracted multures* lay. Bell's Pr., 1017–18.

*Munus publicum.*
A public office.

**Murmur.**
To murmur a judge is to slander him. Hume, i., 406.

**Mutual gable.**
In certain circumstances A may build an end wall of his house, as to half, over the boundary between him and the unbuilt land of X. If X builds he becomes a common owner of this *mutual gable* on paying one-half the cost of erection.

*Mutuum.*

A contract by which fungibles are lent without payment on the understanding that a like amount of the same will be restored at an agreed date.

# N

**Narrative.**

The narrative of a deed (*anglice*, recitals) sets out the names of grantor and grantee and the cause of granting.

**Natural use.**

That use of property which, if due care is taken, does not render the user liable for harm done. Unfortunately the criterion for distinguishing natural from unnatural is not clear. See Glegg on Reparation, 3rd Ed., 305.

**Negative prescription.**

See *Prescription*.

**Negative servitude.**

See *Servitude*.

**Negligence.**

Failure in a duty to shew care towards one to whom such a duty is owed.

*Negotiorum gestor.*

One who in an emergency steps in and acts for another who cannot act for himself, through absence or the like. The process is *negotiorum gestio*.

**New trial.**

In civil jury cases one or more re-trials (new trials) may be allowed on the score of irregularities in the preceding trial.

**Next-of-kin.**

The class of relatives entitled to succeed to moveables at common law. Bell's Pr., 1880.

**Nimious.**

A stock epithet meaning vexatious or excessive, used in conjunction with oppressive · in the expression *nimious and oppressive*. See *Oppression*.

*Nobile officium.*

The noble office or duty of the Court of Session; an equitable jurisdiction in virtue of which the Court may, within limits, mitigate the strictness of the common law.

**Nominal raiser.**

In a multiplepoinding (*q.v.*) the holder of the fund *in medio*, when not he but a claimant initiates proceedings, is called the nominal raiser : when the holder initiates, he is called the *real raiser*.

### Non valens agere.

That a person was not fit to act, *non valens agere*, by reason of minority and the like formerly prevented prescription running against him.

### Nonage.

Minority and pupillarity, *q.v.*

### Non-entry.

A casualty (*q.v.*) caused by the death of the vassal, which continued to be exigible up to the entry (*q.v.*) of an heir and consisted of the rents of the feu.

### Notarial instrument.

" A narrative under the hand of a notary detailing procedure which has been transacted by or before him in his official capacity." Formerly much used in conveyancing, being registered in place of the conveyance itself. Bell.

### Nova debita.

New debts. The Latin expression is used to denote debts, the payment of which, although contracted within sixty days before bankruptcy, is not struck at by the bankruptcy law.

### Notary public.

A functionary known throughout European civilization. His duties in Scotland have been of great importance in recording transactions in land and in matters of shipping, bills of exchange, and bankruptcy.

### Note.

A step in Inner House proceedings in the Court of Session used for making an incidental application. Also, the part of a Sheriff Court judgement in which the reasons for the decision are given.

### Notour bankruptcy.

Insolvency which has become public. It is the result of unsatisfied diligence, the Bankruptcy Act, 1913 containing the modern requirements. Notour bankruptcy is a prerequisite in most cases of sequestration.

### Novalia.

Lands brought under cultivation for the first time by monks and not subject to teind. Erskine, Pr. II., x., 3.

### Novation.

The replacement, by agreement, of one obligation by another, the parties remaining the same. See Gloag on Contract, 258.

### Novodamus.

A charter of *novodamus* is used to make some change in the incidents of a feudal holding or to correct a mistake.

**Nuncupative.**
Oral, as contrasted with written : normally of a will. Latin, *nuncupare heredem*, to name an heir publicly before witnesses.

## O

*Ob contingentiam.*
See *Contingency*.

*Ob non solutum canonem.*
On the ground of unpaid feu-duty. Used of irritancy of a feu for this reason. *Canonem* is commonly mispronounced with the accent on the second syllable.

**Obediential.**
Used of obligations, means imposed by law as distinct from contract : *e.g.*, a parent's obligation of aliment.

*Obiter dictum.*
An opinion expressed by a judge in his judgement upon a point not essential to the decision of the case.

**Obligant.**
The debtor in an obligation. He is in English law the obligor and the creditor is the obligee, a term sometimes used in Scotland also.

**Obreption.**
Obtaining royal gifts by falsehood. *Subreption*, by concealing the truth.

**Obtemper.**
To obey, usually of the decree or order of a Court.

**Officers of State.**
The important officials of state in Scotland. The list has changed from time to time but especially at the Union of 1707. See Green, X., 459, for a full account. At one time the Officers of State represented the Government in litigation.

**Occupancy** or *occupatio.*
A mode of aquiring property by appropriating a thing, *e.g.*, a wild beast, never before owned by anyone.

*Omissa.*
Things omitted from an executry, to remedy which a new grant, *ad omissa*, may be made.

*Oneris ferendi.*
The name given to a servitude entitling the dominant tenement to the support of building on it. Bell's Pr., 1003.

**Onerous.**
Granted for value or consideration, as distinguished from *gratuitous*. The noun is *onerosity*.

*Ope et concilio.*
By help and counsel (strictly, *consilio*), a phrase comparable to *art and part*. Used occasionally, without much reason, by practitioners.

**Open account.**
A debt entered in a book not constituted by voucher or decree. Barclay.

**Open charter.**
A charter (*q.v.*) in which the precept of sasine has not been executed.

**Open doors. Letters of**
A warrant granted in order to permit of poinding property contained in locked places. Opening doors with such warrant was called " Using the King's keys."

**Oppression.**
An offence which consists in using an office or process of law to commit injustice. See *Nimious.*

**Orderly proceeded.**
Regularly carried out. The words were formerly used by the Court as a formal finding in regard to such a matter as letters of diligence. *Proceed* seems to have been treated as transitive.

**Ordinary. Lords**
The judges, five in number, who try cases at first instance in the Court of Session.

**Outer House.**
The part of the Court of Session which exercises a first instance jurisdiction. See *Inner House.*

**Outfangthef.**
See *Infangthef.*

**Outlawry.**
See *Fugitation.*

**Outquite.**
To unburden property from an adjudication by paying the debt which encumbers it. Jamieson. Obs.

**Outred.**
To release from pledge. As a noun, a settlement. Jamieson. Obs.

**Outputter.**
One who passes counterfeit coins. Jamieson. Obs.

**Outside plenishings.**
Implements kept out of doors, as of husbandry.

**Outsucken multures.**
See *Multures.*

**Outwith.**
Outside of, beyond, without.

**Oversman.**
The person to whom falls the duty of deciding, when arbiters differ. Anglice, umpire.

**Overture.**
A formal proposal for a change of church law, made in the General Assembly.

**Oxgang or oxgate.**
A measure of land ; as much as can be ploughed with one ox ; from 12–15 acres.

**Oyess.**
The same as oyez meaning hear ye ; an oyess is the call made as a preface to a legal proclamation.

## P

**Paction.**
An agreement. Archaic.

*Pactum de quota litis.*
An agreement, invalid, by a legal adviser to accept part of what is recovered by action, in lieu of a fee.

*Pactum illicitum.*
Unlawful contract : use of the Latin is common.

**Pains of law.**
Penalty.

**Palinode.**
A written recantation or apology, formerly ordered in the Commissary Court. Mentioned in a note to Stair, I., ix., 4.

**Panel or pannel.**
The prisoner at the bar.

*Paraphernalia.*
Clothes, jewels, and adornments of a married woman, which on marriage remained her own and did not fall within the *jus mariti, q.v.*

*Pares curiae.*
The vassals holding of one superior who attended his court. " In their presence many things relating to the fee and the entry of heirs were transacted." Bell.

*Pari passu.*
Frequently used by lawyers, meaning little if anything more than share and share alike.

**Parole evidence.**
Oral evidence of witnesses, a phrase borrowed from England.

**Parsonage teinds**

Teinds of corn, due to the parson ; in Latin, *decimae rectoriae* or *decimae garbales.* Erskine, Pr. II., x., 5.

**Partial counsel.**

Words descriptive of an objection which could formerly be taken to a witness on the score of his being agent for the party for whom he was called as a witness.

*Partibus.*

The writing of the names of parties, their counsel and solicitors on the margin of a Court of Session summons.

*Particata.*

A rood of land. Archaic.

*Particeps criminis.*

Latin for accomplice, occasionally used in writing and speaking.

**Parts and pertinents.**

Everything connected with or forming part of lands conveyed (except the *regalia*) that is not specially reserved from the grant as, *e.g.,* the *solum* of a lake or a right of pasturage on other lands. Duff, 63. See *Pendicle, infra.*

**Passive title.**

An expression which is used to denote the legal position of one (such as a *vitious intromitter, q.v.*) who through interference with the property of a deceased person is held liable for his debts : in contradistinction to the *active title* of one who can take action to recover debts, having duly entered as heir or obtained confirmation as executor.

**Pasturage.**

A servitude which confers right on the dominant tenant of pasturing cattle on the servient.

**Patrimonial : patrimony.**

Bell's Dictionary defines the latter as " an hereditary estate or right descended from ancestors." But the adjective, which is very common, has a far wider sense and really means " pertaining to property," of any kind. A patrimonial loss is a loss in respect of property, as contrasted with, say, bodily injury.

*Peculium.*

A sum secured to a wife over and above the *paraphernalia.* Rendered obsolete by the Married Women's Property Act of 1881.

**Pejorations** or **deteriorations.**

The contrary of *meliorations, q.v.*

**Penal action.**

An action in which are sought not merely ordinary damages but extraordinary damages by way of penalty. The *Petition and complaint (q.v.)* is an example. Maclaren, C.S.P., 640.

**Pendicle.**
Usually encountered in the phrase *parts, pendicles and pertinents.* (See *parts and pertinents, supra.*) According to Jamieson, pendicle means a small piece of ground, and also anything which is attached to another. It thus seems to extend somewhat the sense of parts and pertinents.

**Penal irritancy.**
An irritancy in which the loss involved by exercise of the irritancy is disproportionate to the value of the right which is secured by it.

*Penuria testium.*
Lack of witnesses ; its significance was that it sometimes justified the calling of witnesses, otherwise incompetent, in times when absolute disqualification of witnesses was commoner than now.

**Perambulation.**
An obsolete judicial proceeding used to decide questions as to disputed marches.

**Perduellion.**
An obsolete name for treason.

**Peremptory.**
An epithet applied to the *defences* in an action, *quae perimunt causam*—which destroy or put an end to the pursuer's case— a defence on the merits as opposed to *dilatory defences.*

*Persona standi in judicio.*
The right of all enjoying full rights of citizenship and who are *sui juris,* to vindicate and defend their rights in a court of law.

**Personal bar, or personal exception.**
A plea in defence based on this that the other party has so spoken or acted as to induce a reasonable belief in a state of matters upon the faith of which the defender has acted to his prejudice, the pursuer not being permitted to gainsay the inference to be drawn from his words or conduct. The English term is estoppel.

*Per subsequens matrimonium.*
Legitimisation of a bastard is effected by the subsequent marriage of its parents.

**Pertinents.**
See *Parts and pertinents.*

**Petition and complaint.**
The procedure in the Court of Session where the remedy sought is a criminal or quasi-criminal one, as against officers of court for màlversation. Maclaren, C.S.P., 914.

**Petitory action.**
An action in which the Court is asked to decree payment or performance.

**Pickery.**
Obsolete term for a trifling theft.

**Pit and gallows.**
See *Fossa*.

**Plack bill.**
The bill on which summonses and letters of diligence proceeded. It was so-called because paid for by *plack*, a copper coin of small value.

**Plat.**
Means either the scheme, or the body in charge of the scheme, devised for the territorial organisation of the Church after the Reformation and for the provision of stipends. Murray.

*Plagium.*
The stealing of a human being.

**Plea in bar of trial.**
A preliminary plea in a criminal case (as, *e.g.*, of present insanity) which, if successful, puts an end to the proceedings.

**Plea-in-Law.**
A short legal proposition at the end of a pleading shewing exactly the relief sought and why.

**Pleas of the Crown.**
See *Crown, Pleas of the, supra.*

**Plead.**
(i) To argue a case in Court : (ii) to argue a case on paper, as in the condescendence in an action ; hence the expression " the pleadings " for the papers or record in a case.

**Plegius.**
Archaic word for cautioner.

**Plough-gate.**
See *Carrucate*.

*Pluris petitio.*
Asking in an action more than is due.

**Poind.**
To take a debtor's moveables by way of execution. *To poind the ground* is to take the goods on land in virtue of a real burden possessed over the land. The word is pronounced *pind*.

**Policies.**
The grounds in which a house is situated.

65

E

**Poors' roll.**
A roll or list of the causes in which one of the parties is enjoying free legal help.

**(i) Porteous or portuous roll, (ii) traistis.**
(i) A roll or list, now obsolete, containing the names of accused persons to be tried before the circuit courts, and (ii) the list of crimes with which they were charged. The *portuous clerks* had the duty of collecting information concerning crimes. Obs.

**Portioner.**
The proprietor of a small feu. And see *Heirs-portioners*.

**Possession.**
Detention of a thing with the intention to hold it as one's own or for one's own benefit.

**Possessory action.**
An action founded on possession and used for holding or recovering possession.

**Power of Attorney.**
A power given to X by A to act for him. An English term, but now much used, the true Scottish term being *factory* or *commission*. Bell.

*Praeceptio hereditatis.*
The acceptance from his predecessor by an heir-apparent of heritage to which he would succeed as heir, constituting a passive title, *q.v.*

*Praecipuum.*
A right which, being by its nature indivisible (as the right to a peerage or a mansion-house) goes to the eldest and not to all heirs-portioners jointly.

**Praedial.**
As applied to servitudes, means those affecting land : as applied to teinds, it means produced by the land, which actually means all teinds. See Erskine, Pr. II., x. 5.

*Praepositura.*
The managership of a married woman in domestic matters (she is *praeposita rebus domesticis*), entitling her to pledge her husband's credit for necessaries.

*Praevento termino.*
An obsolete action in the Court of Session resorted to for preventing delay by a suspender. Bell.

*Precariae.*
Agreements by which proprietors gave their lands to the church and received them back on payment of a rent. Bell.

*Precarium.*
A loan which can be recalled at will. Hence *precario*, at will.

**Precept.**
A warrant or authority granted by a judge or other person having power in the circumstances ; occurring in such expressions as *precept of arrestment, of clare constat, of sasine* (the warrant for infeftment of a vassal given by a superior to his bailie), *of poinding, of warning.*

**Precognition.**
The investigation of witnesses by a procurator-fiscal ; also less formally, the statement by a witness of the evidence he can give in a case of any kind.

**Pre-emption. Clause of**
A clause containing an obligation by a vassal to give the superior the first offer should he decide to sell his land.

**Preliminary defences.**
Another name for *dilatory defences, q.v.*

**Premonition.**
A formal notification to the creditor made by the debtor in a wadset to appear at a place agreed and receive payment of the debt. Stair, II., x., 17. Obs.

**Presbytery.**
A church court next above the Kirk Session, consisting of a minister and elder from each church within a certain district.

**Prescription.**
The passing of a period of time which confers rights or which, regarded from another point of view, cuts off rights or alters the mode of proving them. There are different prescriptions such as *positive* and *negative* (normally of twenty years, formerly forty), *triennial, quinquennial, sexennial, septennial, decennial, vicennial.* Erskine, Pr. III., vii., 1.

**Presence. Hearing in**
The hearing before a larger Court of a case in which the Judges of the Inner House have been equally divided, as to which, see Maclaren, C.S.P., 960 *et seq.* The expression is obsolescent, if not obsolete.

**Preses.**
Chairman, as of a meeting of creditors. Not much used.

**Prestation.**
Performance of an obligation or duty ; *prestable,* means payable, exigible, enforceable.

**Presumptive.**
See *Heir-presumptive.*

*Pretium affectionis.*
A price or value placed upon a thing owing to its owner's attachment to it.

**Prevaricate.**
Wilfully to conceal or suppress the truth.

**Prince of Scotland.**
The title borne by the eldest son of the King of Scotland. The Principality of Scotland consists of lands in Ayr, Renfrew, and Ross. Bell.

**Privative jurisdiction.**
Jurisdiction residing in one Court to the exclusion of others.

**Privileged debts.**
Debts, such as for funeral expenses and mourning, which take preference over the debts of ordinary creditors.

**Privileged summons.**
One in which, from the nature of the case, short *induciae* are allowed.

**Probable cause.**
A cause which is *prima facie*, satisfactory to the intelligence. Glegg on Reparation, 184.

*Probabilis causa litigandi.*
These Latin words are used to mean a *prima facie* cause of action. Reporters on *probabilis causa* are counsel or solicitors appointed to report on whether applicants to be put on the Poors' Roll have a *prima facie* case.

*Probatio probata.*
A fact given in evidence which may not be contradicted.

**Probation.**
Proof. See *Conjunct Probation. Replication. Proof in*

**Probationer. Lord**
A newly appointed judge of the Court of Session while undergoing his " trials," which were essential down to the year 1933. Obs.

**Probative.**
A probative document is one which, because of certain features which give confidence, such as attestation by witnesses, affords *prima facie* proof of its own contents. The principal classes are attested writings and holograph writings.

**Process.**
The writs, forms and pleadings from the first step down to judgement, by which an action or prosecution is brought under judicial cognisance. See Bell.

**Process caption.**
A summary warrant to imprison a person who has borrowed a process which he refuses to return.

**Pro confesso.**

Bad Latin for " as confessed " ; a person is usually held as confessed, *i.e.*, as admitting the claim, when he does not appeal.

**Procuration.**

Really agency or managership, but not used in this wide sense in Scots Law ; practically confined to agency to sign bills of exchange.

**Procurator-Fiscal.**

Literally, the procurator for the *fiscal* or *treasury* ; now the style of the public prosecutor in the Sheriff Court.

**Procurator.**

An old-fashioned term for a solicitor ; sometimes used to-day in a rather formal context.

**Procurator in rem suam.**

An agent who over and above his commission has a material interest in seeing his task carried out. Procuratory *in rem suam* is called in England an " agency coupled with an interest." For *pro-curator*, see *pro-tutor*, *infra*.

**Production.**

An article produced as evidence in court.

**Progress of titles.**

The series of title-deeds, extending normally over twenty years, which constitute a man's title to land.

**Pro indiviso.**

Bad Latin which means, no more than in an undivided state, usually in relation to property held by several persons.

**Propel.**

Of an heir of entail, to anticipate the succession of his heir-apparent by giving him enjoyment of the entailed property before his succession in due course. The noun *propulsion* is also used.

**Procuratory.**

A mandate or commission granted by one person to another as, *e.g.*, a *procuratory of resignation*, *q.v.*

**Propone.**

To advance, put forward, propound.

**Proof.**

In addition to its general meaning, this word has the formal sense of the determination of a case by a judge alone.

**Pro re nata.**

As the occasion arises.

69

**Prorogate.**

(i) To *prorogate jurisdiction* means to waive objections to an incompetent jurisdiction : (ii) To extend the time, as for arbitration, a step in process or the validity of, *e.g.*, a lease.

**Protest. Notarial**

Demands for payment of money due and intimation of assignation may be made by way of a notarial instrument in which the Notary " protests " that the debtor shall be liable on nonpayment to the consequences set forth in the instrument. Bell.

**Protestation.**

Procedure by which a defender in the Court of Session compels the pursuer either to proceed with his action or end it : *protestation for remeid of law*, appeal to the Scots Parliament from the Court of Session. See Stair, IV., 1. 56.

**Protocol.**

A book used by notaries for inserting copies of notarial instruments which they execute.

**Pro forma trial.**

A trial taken in abbreviated form in order to allow of a bill of exceptions being taken to the House of Lords. See Maclaren, C.S.P., 614-15.

**Pro-tutor : pro-curator.**

Persons who act as tutors or curators without right.

**Prout de jure.**

A man who is entitled to prove his case *prout de jure* is entitled to use all means known to the law.

**Proven rental.**

A scheme of the minister's rental proved in a process of augmentation. See under *Augmentation* in Bell's Dictionary for detail.

**Proving the tenor.**

An action of proving the tenor is one in which the pursuer seeks to set up a lost or destroyed document by proof of its contents.

**Provost.**

The chief magistrate in a burgh. He is styled *Lord Provost* in Edinburgh, Glasgow, Perth, Aberdeen, and Dundee.

**Public burdens.**

A quasi-technical expression applied to taxes and the like as they affect land. Bell gives a list.

**Pupil.**

Children up to 12 (girls) and 14 (boys). *Pupillarity* is the state of being a pupil.

**Public right.**
" The technical name given in feudal law to an heritable right granted by a vassal to be held not of himself [as by subinfeudation] but of his superior." Bell.

**Purge.**
Used of an irritancy (*q.v*), it means, to clear off the irritancy by payment or by remedying some failure which produced the irritancy. The noun is *purgation*.

**Purpresture.**
Encroachment by a vassal upon his superior's land which formerly involved forfeiture of the feu. Erskine, Pr. II., v., 37. Also, formerly, encroachment on a public right : see *Slater* v. *M'Lellan*, 1924, S.C. 858.

**Pursuer.**
The person suing in an action.

Q

*Quadriennium utile.*
The four years following on the attainment of majority, during which a minor may seek the reduction of his contracts if made to his *enorm lesion, q.v.*

*Quaequidem* **clause.**
A clause in a charter of resignation (see *Resignation*) by which it is narrated how and why the fee has come to be in the hands of the superior. Menzies, 600.

**Qualify.**
To make out or establish, as in the expression, *to qualify a title.*

*Quanti minoris.*
The action, *quanti minoris* (*literally*, action of, or for, how much of less) is an action for the amount by which purported fulfilment of a contract of sale falls short of what was agreed. The Latin is highly compressed and impossible to translate, literally.

*Quantum meruit.*
Literally, *tantum* being understood, as much as he has earned ; a *quantum meruit* may be sued for where work has been done, obviously not for nothing, but where the amount has not been fixed by contract.

*Quantum lucratus.*
Literally, as much as he has gained ; the phrase involves the idea of gain or profit apart from deserts, which distinguishes it from *quantum meruit.*

71

**Quarter seal.**

A seal kept by the Director of the Chancery of Scotland for the sealing of various commissions and brieves. A fourth part of the Great Seal. See Sources and Literature of Scots Law, 397–98.

**Quasi-contract.**

The name given to a class of obligations in which the legal obligation is inferred from the circumstances : recompense and *negotiorum gestio* are examples.

**Quasi-delict.**

Actionable negligence. Bell's Pr., 553.

*Quoniam attachiamenta.*

The name of an ancient work on the Law of Scotland, derived from its opening words.

**Quot.**

A part—a twentieth—of a deceased person's estate formerly paid as a due to the Commissaries on confirmation.

# R

**Rank.**

To be admitted as a claimant in one's place, as in a bankruptcy ; also, transitively, to admit as a claimant.

**Ranking and sale.**

A process whereby the lands of an insolvent person were sold and the creditors ranked on the proceeds for their claims. Now practically unknown.

**Real action.**

An action, founded on a right of property in something, brought for the purpose of recovering that thing.

**Real burden.**

An obligation which is laid upon lands and not on a person and which, in order to be effective, must enter the Register.

**Real raiser.**

See *Nominal raiser.*

**Real right.**

A right available against the world in general (*jus in re*) as, for instance, a right of property.

**Real warrandice.**

See *Warrandice.*

**Reclaim.**

To reclaim is to appeal against a decision of an Outer House or Vacation judge. Reclaiming is by a *reclaiming motion*, formerly by *reclaiming note.*

**Recognition**

A casualty which obtained in ward-holding (*q.v.*), consisting of forfeiture of his land by the vassal for alienating without the superior's consent. Abolished.

**Recompense.**

A form of quasi-contract (*q.v.*) binding a person, who has made a gain out of what has caused loss to another, to recoup that other.

**Reconvention.**

A right in A to sue X, who is in another jurisdiction, on the ground of X having brought an action against A.

**Record.**

The statements of their respective claims and answers by parties to an action, lodged in court ; when finally adjusted it is *closed* by order of the court and becomes the *closed record* : up to then it is the *open record*. When used in this sense the word bears the accent on the second syllable.

**Records.**

A general expression used in referring to the Register, or the filing departments of the court, and meaning that one which is appropriate to the document under consideration. A deed is said to *enter the records* when it is registered. So too " the Register " is used in a general sense.

**Recourse.**

As a legal term, means the right which a person as the assignee of a right may have, when the right fails, to fall back upon the assignor for relief.

**Recrimination.**

A counter-charge of adultery. In Scotland this forms no defence to the original charge.

*Reddendo.*

The duty or service to be paid or rendered by vassal to superior as provided by a feu-charter : from the words of the clause, *reddendo inde annuatim*. The word is also used as the name of the clause.

**Reduce.**

To annul or set aside by legal process ; hence *reduction* and *reduction-improbation* which is the name given to a reduction when forgery is the ground on which it is sought ; *reduction-reductive* is the reducing of a decree of reduction which has been improperly obtained.

*Regalia.*

Crown rights, some of which, the *regalia majora* as, *e.g.*, the right to hold the seashore in trust for the public, are inalienable, whilst others, the *regalia minora* as, *e.g.*, the right of salmon-fishing, can be the subject of a grant.

**Regality.**

A feudal grant of land " with a high and almost royal juris-diction " (Bell's Pr., 749). Abolished after the '45. A *Lord of Regality* was a grantee of such a jurisdiction.

**Regiam majestatem.**

The oldest of Scottish law treatises. The name is derived from its first words.

**Register.**

See *Records.*

**Register of Sasines.**

After several unsuccessful experiments general and particular Registers of Sasines were established by the Act 1617, *c.* 16. The particular Registers were abolished in 1868. The Register contains a record of all instruments creating and conveying interests in land. The resulting publicity makes it easy for those interested to discover the true legal position of any piece of land.

**Registration for preservation and execution.**

So far as preservation goes the meaning is obvious. Registra-tion for execution is registration in pursuance of a clause in a deed, as a result of which the obligation whose registration is assented to comes to be equivalent to the decision of a court of law. See Duff, 282.

**Registration for publication.**

" Applies chiefly to writs connected with heritable rights and its design is that the condition of all heritable property as re-gards its ownership and incumbrances may be made public and ascertainable by any person at any time." Bell. It is Registration in this sense that forms a corner-stone of Scots conveyancing.

**Regrate.**

To buy food in the market and re-sell at the same market or one within four miles : formerly a crime. Hume, i. 510. See *Forestall.*

**Regress.**

The re-admission, through *letters of regress*, by a superior of his vassal who had divested himself by a wadset (*q.v.*) of his land.

**Reif.**

Archaic term for robbery.

*Rei interventus.*

When A in full knowledge permits X, who has contracted with him, to do something, on the faith of the contract, which is lacking in form and so open to challenge, that is *rei interventus* and it bars A from challenging the contract. Bell's Pr., s. 26, gives the classic definition.

**Relaxation.**

Removal of the incapacity produced by horning ; it proceeded by *letters of relaxation.* Obs.

**Relevant.**

A legal claim or charge in whatever form, is said to be relevant when it can be said that were the facts alleged proved, the remedy sought would be granted. The noun is *relevancy. A plea to relevancy* is an attack upon the relevancy.

**Relief.**

The sum paid by the heir of a vassal on his entering, *i.e.*, becoming the new vassal of the superior. Obs. And see *Bond of Relief.*

**Relocation.**

Re-letting. See *Tacit relocation.*

**Remeid of Law.**

See *Protestation.*

*Remissio injuriae.*

Condonation.

**Remit.**

The transfer of some matter by one judge to another, but more often by a judge to a person named by him as, *e.g.*, to an expert " a man of skill," in order that the latter may inquire and report.

**Removing.**

A removing, or an action of removing, is one by which the landlord rids himself of a tenant whose term has expired or who has incurred an irritancy. The former is an *ordinary*, the latter is an *extraordinary removing.* A *summary removing* is a removing competent in cases where the let is for less than a year, under the Sheriff Courts Act, 1907.

**Rental bolls.**

A fixed quantity of corn paid yearly by the landowner as a substitute for teinds to the person having a right to the teinds.

**Rentaller.**

See *Kindly tenant.*

**Reparation.**

The making good of a civil wrong, usually by an award of damages.

**Repeat (of a summons).**

To bring a summons with abbreviated procedure in answer to an objection by a pursuer that a defence is not competent without a cross-action : this is conjoined with the original action.

**Repel.**
A Scottish Court does not over-rule a plea or an objection, it *repels* it.

**Repetition.**
Repayment of money which for some reason has been paid although not owed.

**Repledge.**
The Lord of Regality could repledge or claim for trial criminals who had committed crime within their jurisdiction, even from the King's judges. See Hume, ii., 30.

**Replication. Proof in**
Evidence allowed to be given by a pursuer after the defender has concluded his proof, where something has come out which could not have been anticipated. Maclaren, C.S.P., 562.

**Repone.**
To repone a defender is to restore him to his position as a litigant when decree in absence has been given against him. Also competent in, *e.g.*, case of failure to lodge documents in appeal to Court of Session.

**Reporter.**
See *Probablis causa*.

**Repository.**
A place where small articles, documents, letters and the like are put for safe keeping.

**Representation.**
(i) See *Passive title*.
(ii) A person is said to represent another when he stands in the shoes of that other, his predecessor, in a matter of succession.

**Reprobator.**
In former times a decree which proceeded upon incompetent evidence could be set aside in an action of reprobator.

**Requisition.**
A demand by a creditor for repayment of a debt, sometimes through the agency of a notary.

**Reset ; or reset of theft.**
The crime of receiving stolen property, knowing it to have been stolen.

*Res communes.*
Things in their nature incapable of appropriation, such as light and air.

*Res furtivae.*
Things stolen and hence tainted, so that property in them remains in the original owner despite subsequent honest dealings.

**Res gestae.**
Literally the things done ; the circumstances. Statements which form part of the circumstances attendant upon an act may often be proved despite the rule excluding hearsay evidence.

**Res inter alios acta.**
A transaction between parties A and X is usually irrelevant to a question between A and B : it is *res inter alios acta.*

**Res judicata.**
A question decided by competent legal proceedings, which cannot again be raised.

**Res merae facultatis.**
A right is *res merae facultatis* when, being exercisable or not at pleasure, it cannot be lost by prescription. See *Faculty.*

**Res mercatoria.**
Commerce : a document in *re mercatoria* may be accepted as valid, though not formal, in order to facilitate commerce.

**Res noviter veniens ad notitiam.**
Information newly discovered, sometimes justifying the admission of new matter in a case, or a new trial.

**Res nullius.**
A thing, in the widest sense, which never had an owner, or which had but has lost its owner.

**Res publicae.**
Things in which the property resides in the state alone, like navigable rivers and highways.

**Res universitatis.**
Things belonging to a corporation, whose use is common to the members.

**Resignation.**
Occurred when a vassal surrendered his estate to the superior, either *ad remanentiam,* permanently, or *in favorem,* where the intention was that the superior should make a new grant, by a *charter of resignation,* in favour of another, probably a purchaser from the person resigning the land. Abolished by Titles to Land Consolidation (Scotland) Act, 1868, s. 17.

**Resolutive.**
Of a condition ; one which brings an obligation to an end if a specified event occurs. A resolutive clause in an entail similarly affected the rights of the heir in possession. See *Irritant.*

**Resting-owing.**

An expression used both as adjective and noun. As the former it simply means, of a debt, unpaid. The resting-owing of a debt is its state of not having been paid.

**Restitution.**

The obligation of restitution is imposed by force of law upon one who is in possession of property delivered by mistake or stolen, or of something found, or of something whose possession is dependent on an event which does not happen. Cf. *Repetition,* where the same principles apply in the case of money. See Bell's Pr., 526 *et seq.* Erskine, Pr. III., i., 5.

*Restitutio in integrum.*

The restoration of a person to the same position as he would have occupied had he never entered into some transaction.

**Respondentia.**

A contract under which money is lent on the cargo to the owner or master of a ship on the condition that if the cargo is lost by sea risk or enemy action the lender shall have no claim : otherwise he is to be paid interest usually higher than the normal rate. Where money is lent similarly on the ship the contract is one of *bottomry.* Bell's Comm., III., i., 4.

**Retention.**

The withholding by one party to a contract of due performance in order to compel the other party to due performance.

*Retentis.*

See *In retentis.*

**Retour.**

Literally, a return : the retour of a service was the verdict of an inquest held pursuant to a brieve issued from Chancery to try, *in primis,* whether the claimant was heir. Dickson, sec. 1100. In its finding the inquest inserted the value of the land according to the new extent (*q.v.*) and this constituted the *retoured duties,* which while the land was in non entry (*q.v.*) fell to the superior. Erskine, Pr. II., v., 15–16.

*Retractus feudalis.*

A power formerly exercised by a superior of paying off a debt due to an adjudging creditor and availing himself of the adjudication.

**Retrocession.**

Re-conveyance of a right to him who gave it. Rarely used.

**Return. Clause of**

See *Clause.*

**Reverser.**

The proprietor of land who has granted a wadset on it. Obs.

**Review.**

Revision by a higher Court on appeal.

**Revince.**

To restore something which has been taken away. Jamieson. Obs.

**Rhind-mart or rynmart.**

Jamieson calls it a "carcass from the herd." Bell says it is applied to any species of horned cattle sometimes occurring as the reddendo in north country charters.

**Rider, or riding claim or interest.**

A liquid claim upon a claimant in a multiple-poinding, which may be lodged in the multiple-poinding itself.

**Rief.**

See *Reif*.

**Reiver.**

Robber: perhaps especially the freebooter who lived on *blackmail, q.v.*

**Rogue-money.**

A tax which was formerly levied in the counties to provide funds for arresting and prosecuting criminals. Abolished.

**Rolls.**

Official lists of cases as set down for hearing. Thus, in the Outer House of the Court of Session there is a *motion roll*; a *procedure-roll*, of cases in which preliminary pleas are to be decided : and formerly a *debate-roll*, now in desuetude, for cases in which there is no issue of fact ; a *long roll* for Inner House cases continued or which for some reason will not at once be decided ; a *short roll*, usually called The Roll, the ordinary list of cases in the Inner House ; and the *Summar roll* of cases in the Inner House which call for early hearing. The *Single Bills* is also a roll of the Inner House, being that in which motions are entered for hearing.

**Roup.**

Auction.

**Rubric.**

Of a statute, the title, once printed in red ; of a reported decision, the head-note.

**Run letters.**

To run letters was to apply in writing to a judge to call on the prosecutor to fix a time for trial : if this was not done within sixty days the accused was set free. Now obsolete, being replaced by simpler procedure. Bell: Erskine, Pr. IV., iv., **48.**

**Runrig or runridge lands.**

A plan of land ownership in which alternate ridges of a field belong to different people.

**Sac and soc.**

A phrase used in ancient grants of land meaning, semble, the right to judge in suits (*sac*) and the district included within the jurisdiction (*soc*).   Cosmo Innes, 55.

**Sanctuary.**

The protection against diligence once enjoyed by a debtor who betook himself to a place of sanctuary, latterly only the Abbey of Holyrood.   Abolished.

**Sasine.**

A seising or putting into possession of land, originally by handing over of earth or stone, and later by registration of an *instrument of sasine* or of the conveyance itself.   English, *Seisin*.   Erskine Pr., II., iii., 15.

**Sasine ox.**

A fee, in substitution for a beast, payable to the Sheriff on his giving sasine to an heir on a Crown precept.

**Saturday's slop.**

Where fishing is by cruive, the trap must be open from Saturday at sundown to Monday, sunrise.   See Bell under *Cruive*. This is sometimes called Saturday's or *Setterday's slop* or *slap*. Slap means gap.

*Scienter.*

This word is sometimes used, in defiance of grammar, to designate the knowledge possessed by the owner of an animal that the animal is savage.

**Seal of cause.**

A grant by magistrates, so empowered by the Crown, by which they created subordinate corporations.   Bell's Pr., 2183.

**Search for encumbrances.**

The process of inspection of the registers, in order to ascertain the validity of a title to land and whether or not any burdens. exist.

**Secondary creditor.**

One who holds a security which is postponed to another or others.

*Semi-plena probatio.*

Evidence somewhere between proof and suspicion which, when existent entitled the party to give evidence on oath (the *oath in supplement*) at a time when parties could not normally give evidence in their own favour.   Usually in affiliation cases. Obs.

**Senator of College of Justice.**
A judge of the Court of Session. The Act 1540, c. 93, so styles the judges.

**Sequels.**
Small quantities of grain given to mill servants under the names of knaveship, bannock, lock and gowpen.

**Sequestrate.**
To render bankrupt. Strictly, it is a man's estate which is sequestrated or set aside for the use of his creditors. To *sequestrate for rent* is to take the furniture, etc., on leased premises to satisfy a claim for rent. *Sequestration* therefore means a process of bankruptcy, except where qualified by the words *for rent*.

**Service ; serve.**
In addition to its meaning, not confined to Scots Law, of formal delivery of process, etc., this word has an idiomatic meaning, viz., a judicial proceeding which transmits the ownership of land from a deceased person to his heir or establishes in a man his title of heir to the deceased ; *special service* establishes the right to be infeft in particular lands, *general service* the general title of heir without reference to particular lands. Bell's Pr., sec. 1824 *et seq.*

**Servitude.**
A burden over a piece of land, the *servient tenement,* whereby the proprietor is restrained in the interest of the *dominant tenement* from the full use of what is his own (a *negative servitude*) : or obliged to suffer another to do something upon it (a *positive servitude*). *Legal servitudes* are imposed by law : *conventional* by agreement of parties. *Praedial servitudes* are servitudes over land : the single *personal servitude* is the liferent.

**Session. Court of**
The supreme civil court in Scotland, with both original and appellate jurisdiction. See Erskine, Pr. I., iii., 7.

**Sett ; set.**
An old-fashioned word meaning, to let. Also as a noun (i) a lease ; (ii) the constitution of a burgh.

**Sett and sale. Action of**
An action by X, a part owner of a ship, claiming that the others buy X's share, or sell their own, or that the ship be sold.

**Sheriff.**
The holder of an ancient judicial and administrative office, once hereditary, when the effective officer was the *sheriff-depute,* now obsolete. To-day the sheriff is either a *sheriff-principal* mainly hearing civil appeals from the *sheriff-substitute* who is

F

a judge with all but unlimited civil jurisdiction and important criminal jurisdiction. *Honorary sheriff-substitutes* are appointed for convenience to relieve the sheriff-substitute, on occasion, of his less important duties. A *sheriff in that part* is a person appointed by the Crown to supply the place of the sheriff in executing process, an original function, and is really a messenger-at-arms.

### Sheriff-clerk.
The principal clerk of the court in a Sheriffdom, now a civil servant.

### Sheriff-court.
The Court of the Sheriff in which crime is tried summarily and on indictment (two years imprisonment the maximum penalty), and civil cases of unlimited value, except divorce and a few others, are heard.

### Sheriff-officer.
A person by whom process is served and diligence carried out in sheriff-court proceedings.

### Shewers.
Persons named by the Court to accompany and shew to the jurors the premises or other object to which a dispute relates, when a view is allowed.

### Side-bar.
A bar in the outer Parliament House at which the rolls of the Lords Ordinary were formerly called.   Bell.

### Side-scription.
This barbarous expression denotes a practice of signing sheets pasted together, partly on one of the sheets and partly on the other : this by way of authentication.

### Signet.   The King's
The Seal of the Court of Session with which are sealed " whatever passes by the warrant of the Session " (Erskine, Pr. I., iii., 39) including summonses and diligence. These were formerly signed exclusively by writers to the signet, a body of solicitors which to this day forms a society apart.

### *Sine die.*
As of a continuation, without fixed date, indefinitely.

### Single bills.
See *Rolls.*

### Single escheat.
See *Escheat, Horning.*

### Singular successor.
A purchaser of heritage or other person obtaining it otherwise than as heir.

*Singuli in solidum.*
See *Conjunct and several, supra.*

*Si sine liberis decesserit.*
" If he shall have died without children " ; these words express the content of two implied conditions in the law of succession : (i) the *conditio si testator sine liberis decesserit,* which means that a man's will, if it does not deal with children, is presumed to be revoked by the subsequent birth of a child ; (ii) the *conditio si institutus sine liberis decesserit,* which means that in case of a bequest to descendants or nephew and niece, their issue, though not mentioned, may take, if they themselves have predeceased. See Gloag and Henderson, 4th Ed., pp. 516 and 529.

**Sist.**
(i) To stay or stop process ; (ii) to summon or call as a party.

**Slains. Letters of**
See *Letters.*

**Sleep.**
See *Asleep.* Most civil actions *fall asleep* after the lapse of a year without any step of procedure having been taken. They must then be *wakened* by a *Minute of wakening.*

**Small debt jurisdiction.**
The jurisdiction of the Sheriff in the Sheriff Small Debt Court in actions involving £20 or under.

**Socage or soccage.**
A form of land tenure in which the vassal rendered agricultural services. Obs.

**Society.**
An outmoded synonym for partnership.

*Socius criminis.*
Accomplice in a crime.

*Solatium.*
Damages given by way of reparation for injury to feelings.

**Solicitors at law.**
A society of solicitors in Edinburgh formerly enjoying an exclusive right to practice in the inferior courts.

**Solicitors before the Supreme Courts (S.S.C.).**
A body of solicitors practising in Edinburgh which was incorporated in 1797. Mackay's Manual, 32.

**Sopite.**
Quash. Archaic.

**Sorn.**
To obtain food or drink by violent means, without payment.
Hume, i., 475. Term obsolete.

**Sowming and rowming. Action of**
An action formerly in use in which it was determined how many
cattle the parties entitled to a common might each pasture
thereon.

**Special case.**
A convenient mode of obtaining the opinion of the Inner House
of the Court of Session on a point of law where the facts are
not in dispute.

**Special charge.**
Letters under the Signet directed to the heir of a person who
had died infeft in land, bidding him enter with the superior.
If he did not, the charger might take the land in adjudication.
If the ancestor had no infeftment but only a personal right, a
*general special charge* was given. See Duff, 302-3.

**Special service.**
See *Service*.

**Special verdict.**
A verdict of a jury not finding " aye " or " no " as to the issue
or issues but making certain findings in fact, to which the Court
later applies the law.

*Specificatio.*
A mode of acquiring property by making a new object, *species*,
out of material belonging to another. Erskine, Pr. II., i., 8.

*Spei emptio.*
The purchase of a chance as, *e.g.*, of a succession.

*Spes successionis.*
An expectancy of succession as distinguished from a vested
right. Connolly & Brown, 165.

**Spirituality.**
See *Benefice*.

*Sponsio ludicra.*
An agreement made in sport as, *e.g.*, a wager, and unenforceable
in Court.

**Spuilzie.**
Taking away moveables from another's possession against his
will.

*Squalor carceris.*
A phrase relating to imprisonment for debt and meaning the
strict imprisonment which a creditor was entitled to enforce.
Obs.

**Staff and baton.**
Symbols used in token of *resignation in favorem, q.v.* Erskine, Pr. II., ii., 10.

**Statute labour.**
Tenants, cottars, and labourers were formerly liable under statute to give so many days' work a year to the maintenance and repair of highways. This duty of statute labour is now superseded by a money assessment.

**Steelbow.**
A custom by which a landlord delivered grain, cattle, tools, and the like to the tenant on the understanding that similar commodities should be given him at the end of the lease. Cosmo Innes, 245 (n). Seemingly from *bow* meaning stock of a farm and *steel* in the metaphorical sense of rigidly fixed, *i.e.*, in amount. See Murray, *sub voce*.

**Stellionate.**
(i) A crime which has no particular name (see Hume, i., 237 and 328), and (ii) in particular, all crimes involving fraud and having no special name (see Erskine, Pr. IV., iv., 41). From Latin *stellionatus*, knavery, cozenage.

**Stent.**
See *Extent*.

**Steward, stewart.**
" The Magistrate appointed by the King over such regality lands as happened to fall to the Crown by forfeiture,. etc." Erskine, Pr. I., iv., 5. A *Stewartry* is a district administered by a steward.

**Steward of Scotland.**
At one time perhaps the greatest of the officers of the Crown, with superintendence of the Household and the Revenue ; the office became merged and lost on the rise of the Stewards to royal rank. Cosmo Innes, 75.

**Stillicide.**
A servitude binding the servient tenant to receive water from the eaves of an adjoining house, eavesdrop.

**Stipend.**
The remuneration of a parish minister based upon the teinds.

**Stirpes. Per**
Succession *per stirpes* takes place where succession to property benefits not only the individuals primarily entitled, but on the decease of the latter, their stock or stirps as well.

**Stoppage in *transitu*.**
The stopping and recall of goods sent by a seller, on his learning of the buyer's insolvency.

**Stouthrief.**

Robbery, Hume, i, 104. But latterly used to mean robbery in a house coupled with violence against the inmates. Term practically obsolete.

**Stress.**

See *Porteous.*

**Submission.**

" A deed by which parties agree to submit a disputed point to arbitration." Bell.

**Substitute.**

A person named as heir who is to take on failure of the *institute, q.v.*

**Subinfeudation.**

The granting of a feu by an owner of land other than the Crown.

**Subreption.**

See *Obreption.*

**Subsumption.**

The second part of the minor proposition in the old form of indictment beginning, " In so far as . . . " and consisting of a narrative of the circumstances of the criminal act in question. Hume, ii., 181.

**Subjects.**

A word commonly used to mean property and usually heritable property. The singular, " subject," is occasionally used.

**Sucken.**

Also called the *thirl* : lands astricted or thirled or bound to a mill where proprietors and tenants had to take their grain to be ground. See also *Multures.*

**Summary.**

As applied to criminal proceedings denotes those taken otherwise than on indictment ; in civil proceedings the *summary cause* is brought in the Sheriff Court to recover not more than £50 ; *summary applications* is a comprehensive name for applications which can be disposed of in a summary manner : as to *summary removing,* see *Removing.*

**Summons.**

Most importantly, the usual form of writ in the Court of Session issued in the King's name and containing a royal mandate to messengers-at-arms to cite the defender to the Court of Session. Maclaren, C.S.P., 291. A summons also originates procedure in the Small Debt Court.

**Superior.**

A person who makes a grant of land to another to " hold of " him as a vassal, in return for a perpetual payment of feu-duty. His estate is one of *superiority*, also called the *dominium directum*. Erskine, Pr. II., iii., 3.

**Supersede.**

Means in Scots Law rather to postpone than to displace, as in the expression, *supersede extract* (see Maclaren, C.S.P., 1103). A *supersedere* is an agreement amongst creditors to sist diligence for a time : also an order of the Court to the same effect. Bell's Comm., ii., 488.

**Superinduction.**

Unwarranted addition to or alteration of a deed. See More's Notes to Stair, p. ccccvii.

**Supplement. Letters of**

A warrant issued by the Court of Session to enable an inferior judge to summon a defender to appear when he did not live in the jurisdiction. Obs. Erskine, Pr. I., ii., 11.

**Supplement. Oath in**

See *Semiplena probatio*.

**Supplementary summons.**

Such a summoms was formerly necessary in order to add parties or change the grounds of action in a case. Now the power of the Court to amend renders this unnecessary.

**Supreption.**

See *Obreption*.

**Surrogate,** also *surrogatum*.

A substitute for something, as, for example, the price of land instead of the land.

**Survivorship. Clause of**

A provision in a will or the like by which the maker, taking into account the possibility that some of the persons benefited may die, makes provision for survivors.

**Suspend, suspension.**

In civil matters, a process whereby diligence may be stayed and also a decree in absence or a decree of a lower court brought under review. *Suspension and interdict* is the process used to stay execution when simple suspension is no longer competent, and also, generally, to prevent injury to any right. Mackay's Manual, 445. In criminal matters, suspension is the setting aside of an improper warrant or a defective decision of a summary court. *Suspension and liberation* is used where the suspender is in prison.

### Suspensive condition.

A condition which suspends the coming into force of a contract until the condition is fulfilled ; sometimes called a condition precedent, the English term.

### T

### Table. To

Bankton's explanation is that at the institution of the Court of Session summonses were directed to be inserted in a table and called in their turn. The phrase is sometimes used of other documents, the users seemingly thinking that the idea is to lay on a table. See Bankton, IV., xxiii., 27.

### Tacit relocation.

Implied re-letting ; the legal principle that where no notice is given to terminate a lease, the lease is renewed for a year (if originally for a year or more) : and for the period of the lease if originally for less than a year. The principle extends to contracts of service. Erskine, Pr. II., vi., 15.

### Tack.

A lease. The term is practically obsolete.

### Taciturnity.

Keeping silence about a debt when a claim would have been natural, leading to an inference of payment. Bell's Pr., 567.

### Tailzie, tailye.

An old name for an entail ; a destination of heritage to a pre-scribed line of heirs, guarded by prohibitions and forfeiture, and only " breakable " on fulfilment of statutory conditions. New creations are incompetent since 1914. Tailzie is also a verb —*to entail*. The z is mute.

### Teind.

Tithe, the tenth part of the annual produce of land.

### Teind Court.

See *Commissioners of Teinds*.

### Temporality.

See *Benefice*.

### Tender.

An offer made during an action by the defender to the pursuer of a sum in settlement. The English tender is an offer before action.

### *Tenendas.*

The clause of tenendas (*tenendas praedictas terras*) expresses the tenure by which lands are to be held. Erskine, Pr. II., iii., 10.

**Tenor.**
See *Proving the Tenor.*

**Terce.**
The liferent of one-third of her husband's heritage given by law to a widow who has not accepted a special provision. *Lesser terce* is the right of a second widow where the land is still burdened with terce and is one-third of the free two-thirds. Erskine, Pr. II., ix., 26, 28.

**Term.**
The date at which rent or interest is payable. Legal terms or term-days are Whitsunday (15th May) and Martinmas (11th November). In England the word means the duration of a lease and also a session of the Court.

**Termly.**
At each term : used as adjective or adverb.

**Testament.**
Will. Confirmation in favour of an executor-nominate is called a *testament-testamentar* ; in favour of an executor-dative, a *testament-dative.*

**Testificate.**
A written statement, not sworn to, used to support an advocation or suspension. Stair mentions it in IV., xl., 3. Obs.

**Testing-clause.**
The attestation clause which sets out the execution of a deed, naming granter and witnesses and date and place of execution.

**Theft-bote.**
The taking of a bribe by a judge from a thief in consideration of acquittal. Erskine, Pr. IV., iv., 15. Obs.

**Thirl.**
See *Sucken.*

**Thirds.**
A third of ecclesiastical revenues which, before the Reformation, the King took and handed over to the Commissioners of Plat in order to safeguard something of their emoluments for the clergy. Bell.

**Thole.**
To suffer or endure : to *thole an assize* is to undergo a criminal trial, after which no other trial on the same charge can take place.

***Tigni immittendi.***
The name of a servitude which permits A to fix in his neighbour B's house a joist or beam from his own. Erskine, Pr. II., ix., 7.

**Timeous.**

An inelegant and unnecessary word meaning in due time, punctual, up to time. Pronounced time-ous, not timmy-ous.

**Tinsel.**

Forfeiture : usually in the phrase *tinsel of the feu*, incurred for non-payment of feu-duty. From *time* or *tyne*, to forfeit.

**Tippling Act.**

A legal slang term for a statute (24 Geo. 2, c. 40) which renders it illegal to give credit for alcohol to a lesser extent than 20/-, thus supposedly discouraging " tippling."

**Title to exclude.**

In an action of reduction this means a title in the defender preferable to that on which the pursuer founds. Bell.

**Title to sue.**

The formal legal right to bring an action.

**Titular.**

Usually, a person who has the title to teinds, like a Lord of Erection (*q.v.*), but strictly one with a title to anything. Cosmo Innes, 204.

**Tocher.**

The marriage portion or dowry of a wife.

**Tolbooth.**

Jail of a burgh.

**Top annual.**

" Mentioned along with ground and feu annuals in 1551, c. 10, as a real burden on houses within burgh." Bell. Skene confesses ignorance of what it really meant.

**Traists** or **traistis.**

A list or roll of the crimes with which persons were to be charged at circuit courts. Hume, ii., 24. Obs. And see *Porteous Roll*.

***Tradito*** or **tradition.**

An expression meaning delivery, occasionally used.

**Transference.**

The process by which an action is transferred to the representatives of a party to it who has died.

**Translation.**

" A deed whereby the assignee of a debt makes over his right to a third party." Bell. Expression obsolete.

**Transportation.**

The technical expression for authorising the erection of a parish church in a different part of the parish.

**Transumpt.**
An action of exhibition in which a judicial copy of the writings exhibited is claimed. Action absolescent. Mackay's Manual, 179.

**Treasurer. Lord**
The officer of state who in pre-Union Scotland audited the accounts of sheriffs and other officers accounting to the Crown. Cosmo Innes, 76.

**Treasure-trove.**
Valuables of which the owner is unknown, found in the ground and assumed to be abandoned.

**Trespass.**
In the limited sense given to it in Scotland, trespass is any temporary intrusion upon the land of another person without his permission.

**Trial.**
The hearing of a case in criminal proceedings and in civil proceedings with a jury. In a civil matter a hearing by a judge alone is technically known as a proof. And see *Lord Probationer* (*supra*).

**Truck acts.**
A series of acts, of which the last is that of 1940, which strike at payment of wages in kind.

*Turpis causa.*
Some consideration in a contract which is immoral in the widest sense.

**Tutor.**
The guardian of children in pupillarity : may be named by parents (*tutor nominate*) ; appointed by Court (*tutor dative*) ; or entitled at law (*tutor-of-law*).


# U

**Udal tenure.**
Land tenure once common in Orkney and Shetland, but now understood to be rare, by virtue of which the owners hold of the Crown for a payment called *skat*, but without the usual feudal incidents of Scottish landownership. Erskine, Pr. II., iii., 4.

*Ultimus haeres.*
Last heir ; the Crown takes as *ultimus haeres* for want of other heirs.

**Ultroneous.**
Spontaneous or voluntary.

### Umquhile.
Former, late, formerly.

### Union. Charter of
A Crown charter which dispensed with the need of taking sasine on each of several pieces of land not adjoining each other. Obs.

### Unlaw.
A transgression of the law, but more usually a fine.  Obs. An example will be found in Mackenzie, I., xix., 15.

### Urban.
Relating to a dwelling-house, rather than in the lay sense of relating to a city, as, *e.g.*, in *urban lease* ; *urban servitude*.

### Uterine.
Born of the same mother but of different fathers.

### *Utlagium.*
An obsolete equivalent for outlawry.

### Uplift.
To take delivery, usually of money, from a place of custody.

### Upset price.
The price at which property is put up for sale by auction.

### Utter.
In regard to forgery and coining, to utter is to put the false writing or coin to the use for which it was meant.

### V

### Vadium.
A pledge.  Obs.

### Valent clause.
" . . . in a retour of special service is that clause in which the old and new extent of the lands are specified."  Bell.

### Vassal.
The owner of the *dominium utile* of land.  He holds the land in some sort as the feudal vassal held of his lord, not as out and out owner, and conditionally on his making an annual payment of a feu-duty.

### *Vergens ad inopiam.*
Approaching insolvency, a condition with many important legal consequences.  See Erskine, Pr. II., xi., 3 ; II., xii., 4 and 17.

### *Veritas convicii.*
Truth of the insult ; a fuller name of the defence to an action of defamation usually summed up as *veritas*.

**Verity. Oath of**
An oath as to the truth of the averment of debt required to be made by a creditor petitioning for sequestration or claiming in a sequestration.

**Vest. To**
To become the property of a person.

**Vicarage.**
See *Teinds.*

**Vice-comes.**
Anciently, the Sheriff.

**Vice. Succeeding in the**
An intrusion on property whereby one enters into possession in the place of a tenant who is bound to remove.

**Vicennial prescription.**
A prescription of twenty years affecting holograph bonds.

**View.**
An inspection of premises, the subject matter of an action, sometimes allowed to jurors before a jury trial takes place.

**Violent profits.**
Penal damages (twice the rent in urban tenements, in rural the highest profit derivable from the land) due on a tenant's unwarrantable detention of the premises when he should have removed. Rankine on Leases, 3rd Ed., 585.

**Vis et metus.**
The Latin name for *force and fear, q.v.*

**Vitious intromission.**
The unwarrantable dealing with moveables of a deceased person, subjecting the offender to unlimited liability for the deceased's debts. Erskine, Pr. III., ix., 25.

**Vitium reale.**
See *Labes realis.*

## W

**Wadset.**
A pledge of lands in security perfected by sasine but with a right of recovery on payment by the debtor, the *reverser* : the creditor was the *wadsetter* : *proper wadset* was where the wadsetter took the rents for the use of the money ; *improper wadset* was where the wadsetter had to pay over the excess of rent or interest. Obs.

**Waif Cattle.**
Stray cattle.

**Wakening.**
See *Sleep*.

**Wand of Peace.**
A baton of a messenger-at-arms "the breaking of which (done by withdrawing a ring from one end to the other) is declaration of deforcement." Barclay, 865.

**Ward-holding.**
A form of feudal tenure in which the *reddendo* was military service. Abolished.

**Ware.**
Seaweed of various species, also called *sea-ware*. Jamieson.

**Warn.**
To notify of the termination of service or of a lease.

**Warning and watching.**
The usual service in burgage tenure.

**Warrandice.**
A clause, usually in a disposition of heritage, by which the granter obliges himself that the right conveyed shall be effectual. *Personal warrandice*, which only binds the granter personally is either : (i) simple, when the granter warrants that he will grant no deed in prejudice of the right ; or (ii) from fact and deed —that he neither has derogated nor will derogate; or (iii) absolute (*contra omnes mortales*), whereby the granter warrants against any cause of loss. *Real warrandice* exists (1) by force of law on an excambion and (2) when other land (warrandice lands) are conveyed in security. Erskine, Pr. II., ii., 11 *et seq.*

**Watch and ward.**
A form of military service formerly exigible by superior from vassal. Abolished.

**Way-going crop.**
The crop, ripe at Martinmas, which the tenant may usually then take on his removing at that, the normal term for removing from arable land.

**Weregild.**
The compensation or assythment due from the slayer to the relatives of a person killed. Term obsolete.

**White-bonnet.**
One who bids at auction for the purpose of enhancing the price.

**Whitsunday.**
A legal term (*q.v*), namely, 15th May. The date notwithstanding, Whitsunday removals take place in virtue of the Act 49 and 50 Vict., c. 50, on 28th May. See *Martinmas*.

**Will (of summons).**
The concluding part of a Court of Session summons, beginning " Our Will is herefore " directed to messengers-at-arms and charging them to summon the defender to appear. Abolished.

**Wind up.**
To liquidate, or put an end to the existence of a partnership or a limited company.

**Writ.**
This word is mainly used as meaning any writing possessing legal significance, rather than in the narrow English sense of a writ of summons.

**Writer.**
An older name for solicitor now, unfortunately, rather rare. For *Writer to the Signet*, see *Signet*.

**Wrongous.**
A wholly unnecessary synonym for wrongful.

## Y

**Year and day.**
" The lapse of a year has several important effects in the law of Scotland, the day being added in *marjorem evidentiam.*" Bell.

## Z

**Zair : also Yair or Yare.**
Jamieson calls it an " enclosure stretching into a tideway for the purpose of detaining (*sic*) the fish when the tide ebbs."

# LIST OF ABBREVIATIONS

**Bankton :** Institute of the Laws of Scotland by Lord Bankton.

**Barclay :** Digest of the Law of Scotland by H. Barclay (3rd edition).

**Bell :** Dictionary of the Law of Scotland by R. (and later) W. Bell (7th edition).

**Bells' Comm. :** Commentaries on the Law of Scotland by G. J. Bell (7th edition).

**Bells' Pr. :** Principles of the Law of Scotland by G. J. Bell (10th edition). References are to Sections.

**Connolly and Brown :** Select Scots Maxims by T. J. D. Connolly and J. C. Brown.

**Dickson :** Law of Evidence in Scotland by W. G. Dickson.

**Duff :** Treatise on Deeds and Forms used in the Constitution, etc., of Feudal Rights by A. Duff.

**Erskine, Inst. :** Institute of the Law of Scotland by John Erskine (2nd edition).

**Erskine, Pr. :** Principles of the Law of Scotland by John Erskine (20th edition).
(This book used to be familiarly known as " Little Erskine.")

**Glegg on Reparation :** Law of Reparation in Scotland by A. T. Glegg (3rd edition).

**Gloag on Contract :** Law of Contract by W. M. Gloag (2nd edition).

**Gloag and Henderson :** Introduction to the Law of Scotland by W. M. Gloag and R. C. Henderson (4th edition).

**Green :** Green's Encyclopædia of the Law of Scotland (3rd edition).

**Hannay, College of Justice :** The College of Justice by R. K. Hannay.

**Hume :** Commentaries on the Law of Scotland respecting the Description and Punishment of Crimes by David Hume (1844 edition).

**Innes, Cosmo :** Lectures on Scottish Legal Antiquities by Cosmo Innes.

**Irons :** Judicial Factors by J. C. Irons.

**Jamieson :** A Dictionary of the Scottish Language by John Jamieson.

**Lewis on Evidence :** Manual of the Law of Evidence in Scotland by W. J. Lewis.

**MacDonald :** Criminal Law of Scotland by Sir John MacDonald (4th edition).

**Mackay's Manual :** Manual of Practice in the Court of Session by Æ. J. G. Mackay.

**Mackenzie :** Laws and Customs of Scotland in Matters Criminal by Sir George Mackenzie.

**Maclaren, C. S. P. :** Court of Session Practice by J. A. Maclaren.

**Menzies :** Lectures on Conveyancing by A. Menzies (1905 edition).

**Rankine on Leases :** Law of Leases in Scotland by Sir John Rankine (3rd edition)

**Shand's Pract. :** Practice of the Court of Session by C. F. Shand.

**Skene :** *De Verborum Significatione* by Sir John Skene.

**Sources and Literature of Scots Law :** An Introductory Survey of the Sources and Literature of Scots Law by various Authors (Stair Society Publications).

**Stair :** Institutions of the Law of Scotland by Viscount Stair (1832 edition).

**Wood :** Conveyancing Lectures by J. P. Wood.